Quality Online Courses: A Writer's Guide

Cover Design:	Shannon Gay
Layout Design:	Sara Ekart
Editors:	Hannah Hanson
	Audrey Kessler
	Sam Stefanova
	Jennifer Thompson

Preface

Online learning is here to stay. This has become apparent over the last decade as more and more students choose to complete their coursework online. While politicians and educational theorists debate the economics and efficacy of online learning, administrators, instructors, and students alike must work through the reality of online learning—its successes, its flaws, and its ever-evolving technology base.

Every day some new piece of software or strategy is touted as the "next best thing" in online learning; but, as the pool of online learning tools grows, one fact has remained the same: Quality learning requires quality instruction. Trained educators everywhere recognize that online learning may change the dynamics of how to deliver instruction, but it doesn't change the principles of sound instruction. Even in an online learning environment, students still need structure, purpose, continuity, and clarity. The challenge facing institutions today is that they know how to create effective instruction on campus but not online.

This book is about empowering subject matter experts (SMEs) who work in fields other than education to become proficient at authoring an online course using sound instructional principles. The book is not riddled with educational jargon. Instead, it's written from a layman's perspective. It covers the basics of what any SME should know about writing an online course.

In my years of serving in online education, I have found that half the battle institutions face with providing a quality online education starts with how they approach course development. My hope is that this book will help schools create a better foundation for student learning in the online environment.

Good luck and happy reading!

Steven A. Huey, MBA
Chief Operating Officer
The Learning House, Inc.

Acknowledgements

First, I would like to thank the hundreds of faculty members and staff, especially Judy Marcum (Dean of Midway College Online) and Anne Marie Hodges (Director of Distance Learning at Notre Dame College) who have worked with us over the years to create quality online courses. You worked tirelessly to create the best online experience for your students for no other reason than to reach thousands of undertrained and underprepared adult learners who need online learning to fulfill their educational goals. This book would not have been possible without your willingness to work with us as we learn—together—the ever-evolving reality of building quality online courses.

Second, I would like to thank the wonderful employees of Learning House, past and present, who lent their knowledge and experience to the creation of this book. For the content of articles, this includes: Elizabeth Dalton, Krystle Feathers, Kim Fountain, Erin Gerdon, Joe Mochnick, Claudia Olea, and Mimi O'Malley. For the book's visual elements (including design, imagery, and layout), I would like to thank Beth Bramble, Sara Ekart, Krystle Feathers, Kim Fountain, Shannon Gay, and Sara Mattingly.

Additionally, I would like to thank the wonderful team of editors who improved the book tremendously by ensuring accuracy, consistency, and continuity: Hannah Hanson, Audrey Kessler, Sam Stefanova, and Jennifer Thompson.

Last, but certainly not least, I would like to thank Steven A. Huey for his vision, relentless follow-up, and concern for the publishing of this book. He deserves significant credit for the final product.

Victoria Alexander
Vice President, Curriculum Development

TABLE OF CONTENTS

TABLE OF CONTENTS

SECTION I
FOUNDATIONS

Chapter 1:
Framework of Understanding

What Is an Online Course?

By Elizabeth Dalton

In the fall of 2008, an astounding 4.6 million students took online courses, representing a quarter of all higher education students in the United States. Online course delivery grew by 17% from the fall of 2007 to the fall of 2008. This rate exceeds the 1.2% annual growth rate of higher education enrollment overall during the same period (Allen & Seaman, 2009).

So What Exactly Is an Online Course?

Most of the online tools we regularly use today emphasize sharing and collaboration among students and instructors. Instructors take advantage of online sites to share course documents, including the course syllabus, PowerPoint presentations, and assignments. Sharing documents online eliminates the need to print documents and spend class time distributing them. Students also have quick access to look up course resources and organize them as necessary while they participate in the classroom. Instructors can choose to share their course documents via a Web tool, such as their own website or blog, or via a campus learning management system, such as Blackboard, eCollege, or Moodle. A learning management system has the added feature of grade book integration.

Some of the most popular learning management systems include Blackboard, eCollege, and Moodle.

With all these options, what defines the type of course that 4.6 million students took online in the fall of 2008? While all the tools previously mentioned allow one to share documents and resources, they also permit students and instructors to communicate about and collaborate on course topics. The amount of time required for online communication and collaboration compared to the amount of time required to communicate and collaborate in a classroom setting helps to define an online course.

The Sloan Consortium has developed the following guidelines for types of online courses (Allen & Seaman, 2009):

PROPORTION OF CONTENT DELIVERED ONLINE	TYPE OF COURSE	TYPICAL DESCRIPTION
1% to 19%	Web-facilitated	Course that uses Web-based technology to facilitate what is essentially a face-to-face course; may use a course management system or Web pages to post the syllabus and assignments
30% to 79%	Blended/hybrid	Course that blends online and face-to-face delivery; has a substantial proportion of the content delivered online, typically uses online discussions, and has a reduced number of face-to-face meetings
80+%	Online	Course in which most or all the content is delivered online; typically has no face-to-face meetings

For our purposes, we will focus on the courses in which 80% or more of the content is delivered online without required face-to-face class meetings. These courses require additional focus and planning in the development of educational content.

Who Teaches Online Courses?

As researchers have studied the number of students taking online courses for several years, they have begun collecting baseline data on the faculty members teaching these courses. A 2008 survey of faculty members at public, land-grant universities showed that 23% of all faculty members responding were teaching at least one course online at the time of the survey and that 34% of respondents had previously taught online. While a perception exists that professors teaching courses online are adjunct faculty members, nontenure-track faculty members, or younger faculty members who embrace technology trends, the data shows that faculty members of all levels of experience and professional standing teach online. Little difference appears in the rates of tenured, tenure-track, and nontenure-track faculty members teaching online or in the rates of instructors who have 20 or more years of experience compared to faculty members who have taught for 5 to 19 years (Seaman, 2009).

WEB-FACILITATED COURSE
Course that uses Web-based technology to facilitate what is essentially a face-to-face course; may use a course management system or Web pages to post the syllabus and assignments.

HYBRID COURSE
Course that blends online and face-to-face delivery, has a substantial proportion of the content delivered online, typically uses online discussions, and has a reduced number of face-to-face meetings.

ONLINE COURSE
Course in which most or all of the content is delivered online and typically has no face-to-face meetings.

How Do Online Instructors Develop and Deliver Their Content?

While many institutions have begun to offer training on how to use educational technology or a learning management system to facilitate an online course, guidance in the development of these courses still is necessary. The preliminary data shows that mid-career, tenure-track faculty members develop courses (Seaman, 2009). As online education continues to grow, more faculty members will be tasked with creating an online course for their institution—and as those mid-career faculty members are tapped to produce these courses, more guidance and professional development will become necessary.

References

Allen, I. E., & Seaman, J. (2009). *Learning on demand: Online education in the United States*. Babson Park, MA: Babson Survey Research Group.

Seaman, J. (2009). *Online learning as a strategic asset: Volume 2. The paradox of faculty voices: Views and experiences with online learning*. Washington, DC: Association of Public and Land-Grant Universities.

Approaches to Online Courses

By Claudia Olea

Most online courses begin as an alternative delivery format to face-to-face courses. When you translate a face-to-face course into an online course, you will encounter similarities and differences between the two environments. The preparation of an online course, for example, requires more up-front planning and project management. Course components that need special attention in an online setting include the syllabus, lectures, study guides, nongraded and graded assignments, quizzes, and exams. For a face-to-face setting, most instructors create a syllabus for the term and then change the schedule according to how the course progresses. In an online setting, however, instructors must estimate beforehand how many lesson activities their students can handle per lesson, unit, or week. One of the most imperative and difficult components extracted from a face-to-face classroom setting is the lecture. While some instructors prepare a lecture for the face-to-face setting and modify the lecture according to student questions on the discussed material, an online setting requires instructors to prepare a lecture similar to one that would be used in a face-to-face setting, anticipate questions that may arise, and try to cover those topics as well. An online course requires this two-faceted approach because the aim is to give students more independence in their study. A common mistake many online instructors make is having the lessons rely too heavily on the required textbook for the course. Students also want to listen to you, the subject matter expert, who has the knowledge that can fill in the gaps from textbooks and outside lesson activities. Keep this in mind as you prepare lectures that reflect the specific knowledge and expertise you bring to the classroom.

Most instructors tend to embrace their online courses as their own. While this practice is highly encouraged, you should consider a different approach if you are both the instructor for and the author of the course. Oftentimes an institution will approach you to write an online course because the institution has not previously offered the course, and you are the subject matter expert on the topic. As you write the online course, always consider that the course is likely to serve as the blueprint for other instructors to use in their classrooms and that you may not even teach the course yourself.

OVERPERSONAL-IZATION
Making a course too specific to a certain instructor, term, or institution so that others cannot easily reuse the course.

SYLLABUS
Podium from which the instructor communicates his or her policies and those of the institution along with due dates and any other course requirements.

INSTRUCTIONAL DESIGNER
The member of an online course team who manages course production and suggests options regarding course materials that instructors may not have considered while writing the course.

TECHNOLOGIST
The member of an online course team who builds a course on the online platform and who may also create different media pieces for the course.

Instructors who also write their courses often make two mistakes: They personalize the courses too much and do not use the different settings that the online platform offers. Some examples of **overpersonalization** include using first person voice in lecture content, asking students to email assignments to the instructor's personal email address, and placing exact due dates within the content of assignments and not within the assignments' functional settings. Some best practices to keep in mind while writing an online course include making the lectures, assignments, and assessments general but informative; using second or third person voice for lecture content; and setting due dates within the online course's functional settings and not within the content of the course so that each time the course is taught, dates within the content must be revised.

You can personalize the course through your syllabus. The **syllabus** is the podium from which you communicate your policies and those of the institution along with due dates and any other course requirements. You should realize, however, that the syllabus you create is likely to serve as the blueprint for the syllabi of future sessions of the course.

As the author of an online course, you must take into consideration student perceptions. To do so, always include course objectives and outcomes, and ensure that the course materials address the course objectives. Some questions to ask yourself regarding student perceptions include the following:

1. Are the course objectives measurable and clearly stated, particularly in the syllabus?
2. Are the lesson objectives measurable and clearly stated for each lesson, and do they meet the course objectives?
3. Does each lesson have an introduction that gives an overview of what students should expect from that lesson?
4. Does the lecture content bridge the comprehension gap left after students have finished their reading assignments and reviewed the Internet resources for each lesson?
5. Do study guides and other tools reinforce what students learn each lesson?
6. Do the assessments, such as quizzes, measure students' performance and provide automatic feedback?
7. Are the course materials modular so that students can easily navigate through the course?
8. Is the course design aesthetically pleasing?

As you write your online course, a team will work with you on the different components of the course materials. An **instructional designer** manages the project and suggests options you may not have considered while writing the course. In turn, the instructional designer works with **technologists** to build your course on the online platform; these technologists also may create different media pieces for your course. You are encouraged to remain in contact with your program coordinator and instructional designer about the progress of the project and to solve any problems with course creation. Depending on whether you are also assigned to teach the course you are writing, the instructional designer will work with other team members with whom you may or may not interact, including an account manager who works with your institution's administration, a customer service representative who handles your requests and functionality problems during the term, and a trainer skilled in the learning management system used for the course.

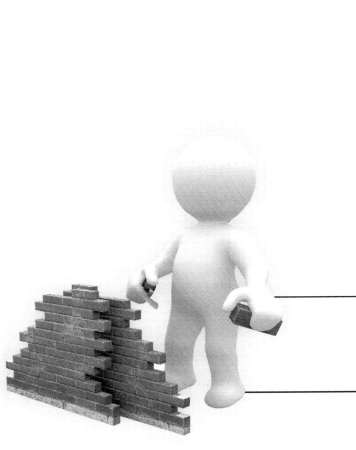

Chapter 2:
Applicable Theories to
Online Course Design

ADULT LEARNING THEORY
The idea that adults need to recognize the significance and purpose of the material they learn so they can learn it most effectively.

ANDRAGOGY
Theory of adult learning that says that adult learners are self-directed, purpose-oriented, internally motivated, and desire relevancy.

PEDAGOGY
The art and science of helping children learn.

Adult Learning Theory

By Erin Gerdon

Adult learning theory is based on the concept that adults need to recognize the significance and purpose of the material they learn so they can learn it most effectively. Today's online learners demonstrate learning characteristics similar to those of adult learners. One of the best known adult learning theories, andragogy, creates a firm foundation for online course design.

Andragogy

Malcolm Knowles developed the theory of **andragogy** almost 40 years ago. He originally distinguished the concept of adult learning from pedagogy, the art or profession of teaching, when he advanced previously held assumptions about adult learners (Merriam, Caffarella, & Baumgartner, 2007):

1. As people mature, their self-concept moves from that of a dependent personality toward that of a self-directed human being.
2. Adults accumulate a reservoir of experience, which is a rich resource for learning.
3. The readiness of adults to learn is closely related to the developmental tasks of their social roles.
4. Time perspective changes as people mature, evolving from the future application of knowledge to the immediate application of knowledge. Thus, adults are more problem-centered than subject-centered in learning.
5. The most potent motivations for adult learners are internal rather than external.
6. Adults need to know why they need to learn something.

Critics have long raised questions about whether andragogy is a proven theory. They have argued the validity of Knowles' assumption regarding the richness of adult experience for application to learning (i.e., that older adults have a richer resource for learning because they have more experiences from which to draw). Moreover, critics have argued that younger people in particular circumstances may have led richer lives than their adult counterparts. As a result of this scrutiny, Knowles redefined his original view of andragogy to make it more situation-specific and not exclusive to adults (Merriam, Caffarella, & Baumgartner, 2007). Andragogy, however, continues as the best-known model for adult learning and differs significantly from its related learning theory, pedagogy.

Pedagogy vs. Andragogy

Pedagogy is commonly defined as the profession, science, or theory of teaching. Knowles further defined pedagogy to ensure a stark contrast with andragogy. According to Knowles, **pedagogy** is not just the general profession, science, or theory of teaching; it is the art and science of helping children learn. Andragogy, when regarded as Knowles originally intended it (i.e., as a set of assumptions), serves as a continuing model for adult education. Neither pedagogy nor andragogy serve as the answer to learning theory; instead, both are components in shared knowledge (Merriam, Caffarella, & Baumgartner, 2007).

Other Models of Adult Learning Theory

Although it is the best-known theory of adult learning, andragogy is not the only theory of adult learning. Three additional theories to consider include McClusky's theory of margin, which precedes andragogy and connects the learner's current life situation to learning; Illeris' three dimensions of learning model, which focuses on the learning process itself (specifically cognition, emotion, and society); and Jarvis' learning process, which has a philosophical, psychological, and sociological base.

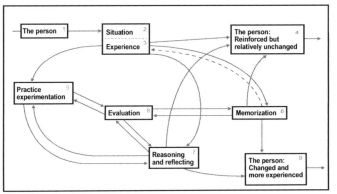

Figure 1. Jarvis' learning process.

Andragogy and Course Design

According to Mary Rose Grant (2010) of Saint Louis University, instructors, facilitators, course designers, and developers must recognize the application of adult learning theories to create comprehensive learning environments that meet the needs of their adult learners.

SELF-DIRECTED
The idea that the online learning environment is learner-centered as opposed to teacher-directed.

PURPOSE-ORIENTED
The idea that adult learners have either professional or personal goals when they enroll in a particular program or course.

INTERNAL MOTIVATORS
Factors such as self-esteem, social status, and self-satisfaction that motivate adult learners to learn.

RELEVANCY
The idea that adult learners need to know why they are learning something and how it might add value to their lives.

LEARNING OBJECTS
Content that comprises a course, including assignments and assessments in a variety of visual and audio formats.

Knowles' andragogy presents a solid starting point for course design and the application of best practices to online courses. Grant (2010) also stated that many of the assumptions that Knowles advanced through andragogy provide the characteristics of online learners: that they are self-directed, purpose-oriented, internally motivated, and need relevancy (p. 19).

Assumption: Adult Learners Are Self-Directed
Self-directed refers to a learning environment that is learner-centered as opposed to teacher-directed. An online course should be learner-centered. Students should be able to use the technology and resources provided (from the course designer) to facilitate self-directed discovery and learning. Learning activities to consider include Web links provided as additional resources for each lesson, weekly Web searches with student results discussed in a chat session or discussion forum, and case studies with varied levels of participation that allow students to move ahead or return to modules when needed.

Assumption: Adult Learners Are Purpose-Oriented
Purpose-oriented refers to the idea that adult learners have goals when they enroll in a particular program or course. These goals may be professional or personal, but they always relate to learning how to effectively manage one's current life situation. To provide an opportunity for adult learners to match their goals with course content, supply them with a detailed course syllabus. A detailed syllabus lists the course goals, learning outcomes, and learning objectives that align with the course assignments and assessments. Also, provide a chat session or discussion forum where students can introduce themselves, discuss their expectations for the course, and offer their knowledge and experiences. This activity, if set up during the first few days of the course, will immediately engage adult learners, allowing them to relate the course to their past and current life experiences. To build on activities for self-direction, consider integrating a problem-solving activity that incorporates a previously developed weekly Web search, outlines a real-life task, and correlates to a learning objective.

Example: An instructor for a general biology course has developed a Web search for the scientific method. Students must find two websites that provide beneficial information on the scientific method. Students must then provide the reasoning for their choices and respond to two other students' posts.

You can easily enhance this Web search activity. For example, in addition to fulfilling the requirements given in the previously stated example, students could be asked to apply the scientific method to solve a current and ongoing problem in their community or workplace. The addition of this requirement makes the activity appeal more to adult learners because it gives the activity a real-life application that should align with a higher-order learning objective.

Assumption: Adult Learners Are Internally Motivated

Adult learners are driven to learn for internal reasons as opposed to external ones. **Internal motivators** may include self-esteem, social status, and self-satisfaction. To meet the needs of adult learners through internal motivation, assess the course syllabus. The previous section stated that a detailed syllabus includes course goals, learning outcomes, and learning objectives that align with course assignments and assessments. To enhance the syllabus and promote self-satisfaction, express high expectations in a course summary and provide weekly timelines and deadlines for students to meet. For example, to encourage students' internal motivator of self-esteem, supply netiquette guidelines that communicate high expectations for online course conduct. Similarly, promote adult learners' internal motivator of self-improvement through the provision of prompt, clear feedback.

Assumption: Adult Learners Need Relevancy

Adult learners want courses that add value to their life circumstances. These learners, however, must recognize the **relevancy** of a course to their own lives, just as younger learners want to know the relevancy to their lives as they constantly ask "why." With adult learners, the course designer must put the content into context. Once the course designer has developed a detailed syllabus, he or she must design assignments and assessments with real-life applications that align with the learning objectives stated in the syllabus. To create assignments and assessments that focus on real-life scenarios, consider course delivery as another aspect of course design. Text lectures involve minimal interaction and apply to only a portion of adult learners if learning style theories are taken into consideration. Therefore, present assignments and assessments in a variety of formats, including articles from websites, podcasts, PowerPoint presentations, and Web quests. The provision of **learning objects** in a variety of formats makes the learning experience relevant to adult learners because they must use skills needed in their employment situation or in their personal lives.

Adult learning theory is based on the concept that adults need to recognize the significance and purpose of the material they are learning so they can learn it most effectively. Today's online learners demonstrate learning characteristics similar to those of adult learners. A foundational knowledge in andragogy can help to establish the groundwork for an online course. Self-directed and purpose-oriented courses that contain relevant material and coursework appeal to both adult and online learners.

References

Grant, M. (2010). Application of adult learning theory in distance learning. In W. Ritke-Jones (Ed.), *Virtual environments for corporate education: Employee learning and solutions* (p. 14-32). Hershey, PA: Business Science Reference.

Merriam, S., Caffarella, R., & Baumgartner, L. (2007). *Learning in adulthood: A comprehensive guide* (3rd ed.). San Francisco: Jossey-Bass.

KEY TERMS

LEARNING STYLE
One's preferred method of gathering, organizing, and thinking about information; one's approach to the processing of information

INFORMATION PROCESSING-BASED LEARNING STYLE
Learning theory that evaluates students' cognitive approaches to comprehending and incorporating information and differentiates the way students may sense, perceive, solve problems, organize, and remember information.

PERSONALITY-BASED LEARNING STYLE
Learning theory that analyzes the impact of students' personalities on their approach to incorporating information.

Learning Styles

By Erin Gerdon

A **learning style** is a person's preferred method of gathering, organizing, and thinking about information (Fleming & Baume, 2006). Learning style models have evolved over the past couple of decades. With this evolution, educators continue to focus their curriculum planning on the idea that students learn in different ways. Similarly, no single approach to teaching works for every student in a classroom. The Kolb experiential learning theory, the VARK model, and the Dunn and Dunn learning style model are three of the numerous learning style models applied throughout classrooms today. Developers of online courses therefore should consider varied learning styles to ensure that the courses meet a variety of learning needs.

What Is a Learning Style?

Theories that students learn and study differently are based on an individual's approach to the processing of information. Students can absorb information in a variety of ways; therefore, learning styles are categorized into three groups: information processing-based, personality-based, and multidimensional/instructional-based (Mokhtar, Majid, & Foo, 2008).

Information processing-based learning styles evaluate students' cognitive approaches to comprehending and incorporating information. A learning style within this category differentiates the way students may sense, perceive, solve problems, organize, and remember information. A **personality-based learning style** analyzes the impact of students' personalities on their approach to incorporating information. A learning style within this category measures the reaction of students in various learning situations. **Multidimensional/instructional-based learning styles** evaluate the type of learning environment students want (Mokhtar, Majid, & Foo, 2008).

Kolb Experiential Learning Theory

David A. Kolb, in conjunction with Roger Fry, developed the **Kolb Experiential Learning Theory**, in which learning is a continuous process that involves, in sequential order, concrete experience (CE), reflective observation (RO), abstract conceptualization (AC), and active experimentation (AE) (Hawk & Shah, 2007).

MULTI-DIMENSIONAL/ INSTRUCTIONAL-BASED LEARNING STYLE
Learning theory that evaluates the type of learning environment students want.

KOLB EXPERIENTIAL LEARNING THEORY
Experiential learning style model whereby learning is a continuous process that involves (in sequential order) concrete experience, reflective observation, abstract conceptualization, and active experimentation.

As shown in Figure 1, four basic learning styles emerge from Kolb's theory: converger (AC/AE), diverger (CE/RO), assimilator (RO/AC), and accommodator (AE/CE).

Convergers have strong deductive reasoning and problem-solving skills, tend to be practical in the application of ideas, and have narrow or focused interests.

Divergers tend to be imaginative, are skilled in seeing scenarios from different viewpoints, and have broad interests. Assimilators tend to excel at inductive reasoning, enjoy creating theoretical models, and are interested in abstract concepts rather than people.

Accommodators tend to be risk-takers, perform well under pressure, and enjoy solving problems intuitively.

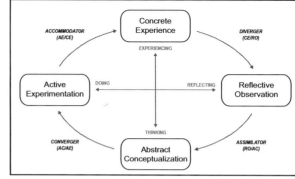

Figure 1. Kolb experiential learning model.

CONCRETE EXPERIENCE	REFLECTIVE OBSERVATION	ABSTRACT CONCEPTUALIZATION	ACTIVE EXPERIMENTATION
Lecture examples, problem sets, readings, films, simulations, laboratories, observations, fieldwork	Thought questions, brainstorming, discussions, logs, personal journals	Lecture, papers, analogies, text readings, projects, model building, model critiques	Lecture examples, laboratories, case studies, homework, projects, fieldwork

Table 1. Activities that accommodate Kolb learning processes. Kolb (1984); Svinicki and Dixon (1987).

Table 1 presents example activities that are suitable for each Kolb learning process. For example, if you are a diverger, Kolb's theory suggests that the learning processes of concrete experimentation and reflective observation will assist you most. Activities to consider include readings, lecture examples, thought questions, and personal journals.

The VARK Model

The **VARK model** serves as a sensory guide to learning styles. VARK stands for visual (V), aural (A), read/write (R), and kinesthetic (K), the four perceptual modes covered in the model. The VARK model provides individuals with opportunities for learning through one or more preferred perceptual modes. Figure 2 illustrates the VARK model and shows the sensory modes included within each learning style. The VARK questionnaire presents 16 statements that describe different scenarios; individuals then choose one of four action options that best represents the specific one he or she would most likely exhibit. Finally, the actions correspond with a perceptual mode, or learning style, within the VARK model.

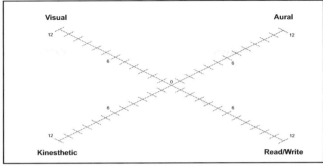

Figure 2. VARK learning model.

VISUAL	AURAL	READ/WRITE	KINESTHETIC
Diagrams, graphs, colors, charts, written texts, different fonts, spatial arrangement, designs	Debates, arguments, discussions, conversations, audio tapes, video and audio, seminars, music, drama	Books, texts, handouts, reading, written feedback, note taking, essays, multiple choice, bibliographies	Real-life examples, guest lecturers, demonstrations, physical activity, constructing, role-play, working models

Table 2. Activities that accommodate VARK learning styles. Fleming (2001).

Table 2 provides accommodating activities within the different learning methods for the four VARK learning styles. Individuals who have a visual preference may benefit from graphs, charts, written lectures, and a variety of fonts. Individuals who have an aural preference may benefit from recorded lectures, video and audio resources, and music. Individuals who have a read/write preference may benefit from multiple choice, script notes, downloadable lectures, and textbooks. Individuals who have a kinesthetic preference may benefit from constructing models, demonstrations, and role-playing (Hawk & Shah, 2007).

VARK MODEL
Sensory learning style model that focuses on visual, aural, reading and writing, and kinesthetic learning methods.

DUNN AND DUNN LEARNING STYLE MODEL
Model that suggests that five key dimensions (i.e., environmental, emotional, sociological, physiological, and psychological) differentiate learning styles.

	20	30	40	50	60	70	80	
Prefers quiet								Prefers sound
Prefers dim light								Prefers bright light
Prefers cool environment								Prefers warm environment
Prefers informal design								Prefers formal design
Low motivation								High motivation
Low persistence								High persistence
Low responsibility								High responsibility
Doesn't like structure								Wants structure
Prefers learning alone								Prefers learning with others
No authority figures present								Wants authority figures present
Doesn't learn in several ways								Learns in several ways
Low auditory learner								Prefers auditory learning
Low visual learner								Prefers visual learning
Low tactical learner								Prefers tactical learning
Low kinesthetic learner								Prefers kinesthetic learning
Doesn't prefer intake								Prefers intake
Prefers evening								Prefers morning
Doesn't prefer late morning								Prefers late morning
Doesn't prefer afternoon								Prefers afternoon
Doesn't prefer mobility								Prefers mobility

Figure 3. Dunn and Dunn learning style model survey.

Dunn and Dunn Learning Style Model

The **Dunn and Dunn learning style** model suggests that five key dimensions—environmental, emotional, sociological physiological, and psychological—differentiate learning styles. Within these five key dimensions lie several elements that benefit each respective dimension. Table 3 lists learning style elements that correspond directly to each key dimension. In addition to listing these elements, the table provides key questions to help guide instructors to a more focused set of elements.

The Dunn and Dunn learning style model survey covers all five key dimensions and their respective learning style stimuli. Figure 3 reflects the two ends of the score range; individuals can score from 20 to 80, with a score of 40 to 60 representing a balanced preference and a score of either 20 to 40 or 60 to 80 representing a stronger preference (Dunn, 2000).

DIMENSION	ELEMENTS	KEY QUESTIONS
Environmental	Sound, light, temperature, seating design	Do students prefer a noisy, busy, well-lit, warm environment or a quiet, subdued, cooler environment? Should the learning environment be formal (e.g., desks and chairs) or informal (e.g., pillows)?
Emotional	Motivational support, persistence, individual responsibility, structure	Do students need a lot of emotional support? Will they persist on learning tasks? Can they assume individual responsibility? Do they need lots of structure?
Sociological	Individual, pairs or teams, adult, varied	Do students learn best alone or working with someone? How much guidance from adults do they want or need?
Physiological	Perceptual, intake, time, mobility	Are students auditory, visual, tactual, or kinesthetic learners? Do students like to snack while learning? When is the optimal time for learning? Do students require freedom to move during learning?
Psychological	Global, analytical, impulsive, reflective	How do students attack problems—globally or analytically? Do students jump into problems or pause to reflect before starting?

Table 3. Learning dimensions.

Learning Styles and the Online Classroom

Research suggests that faculty members in higher education initially adopt a teaching style that reflects their own learning style and/or adopt a teaching method that proved effective during their own education program (Hawk & Shah, 2007). This approach results in faculty members who are unfamiliar or uncomfortable with incorporating various learning style models into their curricula.

It is important to recognize the individual learning styles and needs of individual students. Online instructors usually do no interact with students face-to-face; therefore, they may focus more on the methodology of course delivery than the needs o each student. However, these two foci complement each other. In terms of online course development, all three of the learning style models discussed in this article give examples of accommodating activities for individual students.

A review of the three tables depicting learning style models shows similarities throughout the individual styles. According to the Kolb model, abstract conceptualization activities include written lectures, textbooks, and supplemental papers. Similarly, the VARK model includes these same activities in the read/write learning style, and the Dunn and Dunn model has this preference within the psychological dimension. An online course should include various activities from each learning model. The inclusion o written lectures, audio accompanying lectures, textbook assignments, supplemental papers to read or write, thought questions links to videos, example problems, group sessions, homework, and a comprehensive assignment to tie the course together wi help meet the learning needs of individual students and create a quality online course.

References

Dunn, R. (2000). Learning styles: Theory, research, and practice. *National Forum of Applied Educational Research Journa 13*(1), 3-22.

Fleming N. D. (2001). *Teaching and learning styles: VARK strategies*. Honolulu, HI: Honolulu Community College.

Fleming, N., & Baume, D. (2006). Learning styles again: VARKing up the right tree! *Educational Developments, 7*(4), 4-7.

Hawk, T., & Shah, A. (2007). Using learning style instruments to enhance student learning. *Decision Sciences Journal o Innovative Education, 5*(1), 1-19.

Kolb, D. A. (1984). *Experiential learning: Experience as the source of learning and development*. Englewood Cliffs, NJ: Prentic Hall.

Mokhtar, A., Majid, S., & Foo, S. (2008). Information literacy education: Applications of mediated learning and multipl intelligences. *Library & Information Science Research, 30*(3), 195-206.

Svinicki, M. D., & Dixon, N. M. (1987). The Kolb model modified for classroom activities. *College Teaching, 35*(4), 141-146.

SECTION II
TOOLS OF THE TRADE

Chapter 3:
Learning Management Systems in Online Course Design

LEARNING MANAGEMENT SYSTEM (LMS)
Web-based system that enables instructors to create, deliver, and facilitate online courses without the help of any other software or database.

SYNCHRONOUS
Sessions in which instructors and students engage at the same time, as with face-to-face or chat room sessions.

UPLOAD
Feature of a learning management system that allows students to electronically deliver work to their instructors.

The Purpose of an LMS

By Krystle Feathers

As you explore the online learning environment, you will find it as broad and varied as the traditional classroom. While online and traditional courses share many developmental steps, you must carefully consider the format and platform for course delivery when you develop an online course.

Institutions deliver effective, fully online courses via a **learning management system (LMS)**. At the most basic level, an LMS is a Web-based system that encompasses many different aspects of instruction. It gives you the features you need to create, deliver, and facilitate your course online without the help of any other software or database.

Institutions can select from various LMSs based on their individual needs. Although LMS features vary, these systems typically offer instructors the ability to create, store, and deliver content as well as create assessments, such as quizzes and tests. LMSs also provide course communication features, such as forums for threaded discussions, **synchronous** chats (sessions in which instructors and students engage at the same time), and Web mail. In addition, they provide students with the ability to electronically deliver work to their instructors through an **upload** feature. Most LMSs also include administrative features, such as enrollment capabilities for registration, user tracking, and management of data and records.

You create a **course shell** on the LMS to begin building an online course; depending on the system you are using (and/or your personal preference), you can divide the course according to weeks, modules, topics, or content area.

Once you have written a course for the online environment, you can build the course's individual components within the LMS course outline. You likely will create most of your course content and lecture material externally, upload it to the course, and then link it within the course outline. The LMS allows you to upload a variety of external documents to the course, such as text documents (.doc, .rtf, and .txt), PDF files, Microsoft PowerPoint presentations, and images. You also can enter text into a **WYSIWYG editor** to create content pages directly in the LMS instead of uploading external text documents. Regardless of how your lecture material is created (either externally or within the LMS), you will build assignments and assessments directly in the LMS and attach them to an online grade book that aligns with the course syllabus.

Students log in to their course through the LMS, study the lecture material, finish any exercises or activities they have been assigned, and complete their assessments. They can also check the grade book, which keeps track of their scores. Instructors can customize the grade book to meet their individual needs, such as adding participation points for forum discussions.

Major Learning Management Systems

Developers work constantly to upgrade LMSs, adding new features to respond to user demands and advances in technology, updating software for privacy and security enhancements, and acquiring competing companies.

Blackboard, Inc., founded in 1997, undoubtedly is the oldest company that still maintains a large user base. Many consider Blackboard the leader in the development of e-learning tools, specifically the **closed-source learning management system**, proprietary software that you must pay to use and cannot customize without authorization. In Blackboard's 13-year history, it has acquired two other rival LMSs: WebCT in 2006 and ANGEL in 2009.

Currently, Moodle (Modular Object-Oriented Dynamic Learning Environment) serves as Blackboard's chief rival. Moodle is an **open-source learning management system**, which means that anyone can run the system free of charge and modify it to create a more customized platform for delivering instruction. Although the concept of Moodle was first announced in 2001, Moodle 1.0 did not release until 2002—and then another 4 years passed before the release of Moodle 1.6. Since then, Moodle has led the way in open-source LMS development and, as of October 2010, has grown to serve more than 37 million users (Moodle, 2010).

A 2010 survey from The Campus Computing Project (Green, 2010) noted that Blackboard use was falling, while the use of Moodle and other competitors was steadily rising:

COURSE SHELL
The layout of a course on a learning management system in which instructors can divide courses according to weeks, modules, topics, or content area.

WYSIWYG EDITOR
Feature of a learning management system that allows instructors to create content pages directly in the learning management system instead of uploading external text documents.

CLOSED-SOURCE LEARNING MANAGEMENT SYSTEM
Proprietary software that you must pay to use and cannot customize without authorization.

OPEN-SOURCE LEARNING MANAGEMENT SYSTEM
Web-based system that you can run free of charge and modify to create a more customized platform for delivering instruction.

VIRTUAL LEARNING ENVIRONMENT (VLE)
Another term for learning management system; term used primarily in the United Kingdom and other European countries

CONTENT MANAGEMENT SYSTEM (CMS)
Web-based system that instructors can use to create, store, and deliver content but does not contain features related to instruction, assessment, or grades; used primarily for hybrid or face-to-face courses.

The proportion of campus CIOs and senior IT officials reporting that their institution uses Blackboard as the campus-standard LMS has dropped from 71.0 percent in 2006 to 57.1 percent in 2010. Concurrently, Blackboard's major LMS competitors have all gained share during this period. The percentage of campuses that use Desire2Learn as the campus-standard LMS is up five-fold, from 2.0 percent in 2006 to 10.1 percent in 2010. Moodle, an Open Source LMS, also registered big gains during this period, rising from 4.2 percent in 2006 to 16.4 percent in fall 2010. The numbers for Sakai, another Open Source LMS deployed primarily in research universities, have grown from 3.0 percent in 2006 to 4.6 percent in 2010. (Green, 2010, p. 1)

The two other most popular LMSs in higher education are Desire2Learn (D2L) and Sakai. D2L was founded in 1999 as a closed-source LMS. Sakai released version 1.0 of its LMS in 2005 and serves as Moodle's open-source competitor. Sakai includes the same basic functions as Moodle, but it focuses more on research and group projects.

Which LMS an institution selects depends entirely on the institution's specific needs. Each LMS comes with its own benefits and drawbacks, and the choice usually involves much debate and deliberation on the institution's part. The institution must take into account such issues as cost, size (i.e., how many users they expect will enroll and how many courses they expect to offer), the institution's desired purpose, future maintenance, and the institution's technical capabilities.

Other Common Systems
Although people who work in online education and corporate training usually use the term LMS, you may also hear terms such as VLE, CMS, and LCMS.

Virtual Learning Environment (VLE)
The term **virtual learning environment (VLE)** often appears in online education research. Although this may seem confusing at first, VLE is just another term for LMS, and the two systems have the same functionality. Typically, only people in the United Kingdom and other European countries use the term VLE; however, a significant amount of research in online education comes from those countries, so articles and discussions often use the term.

Content Management System (CMS)

An instructor who teaches a hybrid course, or a face-to-face course that uses online components as supplements, may use a **content management system (CMS)**. This system is similar to an LMS, except that it does not contain features related to instruction. While you can create, store, and deliver content with a CMS, you cannot quiz, grade, or assess students with it, and you cannot store data related to grades. The system does, however, meet the needs of instructors who simply want to post documents, such as a syllabus or additional readings, for students to download and read outside of class.

One popular open-source CMS is called Joomla. This system was developed in 2005 and subsequently won Packt Publishing's 2006 Open-Source Content Management System Award (Packt Publishing, 2006) and 2007 Best Open-Source PHP Content Management System Award (Packt Publishing, 2007).

Learning Content Management System (LCMS)

A **learning content management system (LCMS)** focuses more on content than on learners. It does not contain the instruction and assessment features of an LMS, but it does have one capability that an LMS lacks: It allows you to manage and reuse content without duplicating your development time.

Unlike an LMS or a CMS, which allow students enrolled in individual courses to download and review material, an LCMS serves as a back end object repository for learning objects (i.e., "chunks" of content or reusable assets). With an LCMS, you can store learning objects with multiple versions and then select one or more of them for use within various courses. The LCMS then delivers the objects to an LMS, where students can access them. When you need to change individual objects, you make those changes within the LCMS. Each instance of that object then updates automatically in the LMS, eliminating the need for duplicate work in multiple courses.

Where Do You Go From Here?

As the person responsible for developing an online course, you may or may not actually instruct the course; however, knowing the features of an LMS and how it operates will help you develop your course.

LEARNING CONTENT MANAGEMENT SYSTEM (LCMS)
Web-based system that stores learning objects that instructors can arrange and use for multiple courses without re-creating each learning object.

References

Green, K. C. (2010, October). *The 2010 national survey of information technology in U.S. higher education.* Encino, CA: The Campus Computing Project. Retrieved November 22, 2010, from http://www.campuscomputing.net/sites/www.campuscomputing.net/files/Green-CampusComputing2010.pdf

Moodle. (2010). *Moodle statistics: Total known sites.* Retrieved November 22, 2010, from http://moodle.org/stats/

Packt Publishing. (2006). *2006 Open Source Content Management System Award winner announced.* Retrieved January 24, 2011, from http://www.packtpub.com/article/open-source-content-management-system-award-winner-announced

Packt Publishing. (2007). *Joomla! wins Best PHP Open Source Content Management System.* Retrieved January 24, 2011, from http://www.packtpub.com/article/joomla-wins-best-php-open-source-content-management-system

How the LMS Impacts Course Creation

By Kim Fountain

As you think about preparing your course for the LMS you will use, make sure to consider consistency and coherence. Many students find online courses unfamiliar. Creating an environment of trust and instructor dependability is important. You can establish trust if you set clear goals for your students, which allows them to successfully complete tasks the way they would in a face-to-face classroom.

An LMS can help you establish goals and clear objectives for your students. An LMS can also help you maintain a reward and recognition system for students who meet the established learning goals and objectives. As you prepare your course, make sure you consider the tools the LMS offers and how you can use them to give your students the best learning experience possible.

Presenting Lectures

You can make written or recorded materials available to students by uploading them to the LMS. Instructors can do any of the following to record lecture materials:
- Create lectures in Web page resources directly in the LMS.
- Create lectures in Microsoft Word, Microsoft PowerPoint, and Adobe PDF documents.
- Videotape lectures.
- Archive virtual classroom lectures.
- Audiotape lectures.

Web Page Resources in the LMS

Your LMS will provide an authoring tool that allows you to build Web pages and edit **hypertext markup language (HTML)**, the code that structures tags to lay out information as Web pages. HTML editors have two interfaces: One allows you to see the actual HTML markup, and the other allows you to see how the Web page appears to the public. These tools require no programming skills, and they allow instructors to create course content by typing directly into a built-in text editor. You may use the HTML editor to manage fonts, tables, figures, images, charts, and links as well as check for spelling errors. The HTML approach generally works better for Web pages

HYPERTEXT MARKUP LANGUAGE (HTML)
Code that structures tags to lay out information as Web pages.

VIRTUAL CLASSROOM
Software, such as Adobe Connect, that provides real-time voice or streaming video and allows instructors to deliver live lectures as they would in a traditional classroom.

ASYNCHRONOUS
One-way electronic communication (e.g., discussion forums that allow users to post and read messages at any time).

with minimal content, such as a list of reading assignments for the week or a reminder to students about a large project or assignment.

Word Processors

With word processing software, such as Microsoft Word, WordPerfect, and OpenOffice, you can create a high-quality and easily organized instructional product. These programs allow you to add drawings that illustrate key points, add tables that organize information, check spelling and grammar, and provide workable documents for many uses. Word processors can convert documents to HTML, which you then can save as .txt (i.e., text) files and upload them onto a server as Web pages. Saving documents as PDF files makes them uneditable, and it condenses the file size for easy user access. Instructors can use the "Save as PDF" command in a word processing program to convert documents to a PDF, which users can then view on any computer. With PDF files, you can embed specific fonts that users may not have on their computers, such as foreign languages. Embedded fonts will appear to students exactly as they appear in the original document. You can easily upload and link to an LMS any documents you have created with a word processor.

Slide Presentations

The best way to use PowerPoint presentations as self-contained lectures or as supplements to lectures involves the use of a software product that turns PowerPoint presentations into interactive content pieces. This conversion allows students to open and view the presentation regardless of the programs they have installed on their viewing computers. You may also want to consider adding voice-over narration to PowerPoint slides because delivering content in various ways sparks interest among students and adds instructional value. Adobe Connect, Adobe Captivate, and Articulate are a few of the programs that do this type of conversion.

Videotaping

Videotaping best serves instruction that demonstrates techniques or situations in which students must apply what they have learned to a specific instance or scenario. Instructors, however, must use video wisely, keeping the clips short and informative. Otherwise, students will lose interest and not comprehend the necessary material. Videos that have large file sizes may cause issues because students will have more difficulty streaming them, resulting in frustrated students and instructors. You can record videos in a multitude of formats and then upload them to or create a link to them in the LMS and view the material on a Web page. To ensure cross-platform and browser compliance, the MP4 format is recommended.

Online Meeting Rooms

Online meeting room software options, such as Adobe Connect, work as **virtual classrooms**. You should consider using this tool when the addition of real-time voice or streaming video will help your instruction. Online meeting rooms work well for language instruction, conversation-based assignments, lectures, debates, and conversations with students during virtual office hours. Virtual classrooms effectively allow you to deliver live lectures like you would in a traditional classroom. You can upload and organize your content (e.g., PowerPoint slides or images) for display and manage communication in a virtual classroom on both an individual and a group level. In addition, you can record and archive live sessions, making them available for absent students, students who want to review the material, and students who cannot meet in the virtual classroom at a specific time on a specific day. Archived live sessions especially benefit and appeal to students who must complete coursework at night or in the early morning because of their schedules. Archiving lectures via virtual classrooms, however, also benefits instructors because it allows them to complete their work in advance so they can focus more on facilitating their courses than developing course materials while classes are underway.

Audio

A printable script in text format should accompany all audio lectures. The script allows students to read along and remain connected to the material during the presentation. Instructors can upload audio lectures to the LMS in MP3 or MP4 format, or they can publish them to a program that hosts and presents the file in an audio player.

Lecture Supplements

Depending on the frequency and requirements of your lectures, some of your content may come in the form of reference materials, study resources, or resources that provide further reading on core concepts for students who want to acquire more knowledge. Supplemental materials (e.g., PDF articles and websites) for an online course allow students to take control of their education and further their knowledge base.

Some ideas for supplemental materials to accompany your lecture include the following:

- PowerPoint presentations
- Microsoft Excel spreadsheets
- PDF files
- Adobe Flash presentations
- Videos
- Links to external sources
- Reference lists and bibliographies

You should consider using PowerPoint, Flash, and videos when demonstrating procedures and concepts. These multimedia programs present content in aesthetically pleasing and informative formats. You can make PowerPoint presentations viewable in a Flash presenter or print them to use as study guides for students.

Excel spreadsheets effectively supplement finance and accounting courses, especially because students can download specific forms that the instructor used in the lecture. You should consider using Excel for financial assignments, such as organizing expenses.

You can create PDFs from almost any document you want to include as a resource for students. Items you may want to produce as PDF files include tables, articles, case studies, and maps. Students may print these materials, download them, and save them to their computers or view them online directly from the LMS.

Every course should include a comprehensive collection of Internet resources that support the curriculum and reinforce skills. You can add reference links through the Web page function in your LMS.

It is important to acknowledge the source of any direct or indirect quote used in the text, as it creates a more scholarly course.

Bibliographic information for sources, such as websites, articles, and books, enables students to know the source of the information presented, and if desired, they can view the source for further information. Instructors should use a citation style, such as APA or MLA, to include these references.

Peer Learning

Encouraging students to collaborate to achieve goals will help them feel like they belong to a community, which will increase the likelihood that each student will engage with the material. This community atmosphere also increases the likelihood that you will retain students throughout the course and possibly even throughout an entire degree program.

A few LMS components that aid interaction among students include the following:
- Discussion forums
- Online meeting rooms
- Chat

Discussion Forums

When writing an online course, you should think about areas where you can include group interaction. Discussion forums allow students to communicate with each other, which promotes peer-to-peer learning. As an **asynchronous** (or one-way electronic communication) tool, discussion forums allow users to post and read messages at any time. This mode of conversation also allows instructors to archive messages.

Discussion forums organize messages through threads, or topics. Both instructors and students can post messages to existing threads, add new threads to the discussion, and read comments from others. This form of communication allows students to take time to think about the topic before they respond. Some LMSs allow users to include links and images in their posts. Both students and instructors can choose to receive notification of new posts on a discussion forum where they have posted their own comments. The instructor also has the choice of locking, unlocking, and hiding threads. Locking a thread prevents students from posting responses. You may choose to lock a thread so that students can participate in a discussion only after they have reached a certain milestone in the course. You also might choose to lock a thread because it covers the same topic as another thread and you want to contain the conversation within a common thread, the thread was posted in the wrong section, or you want the students to move on to a new topic.

Chat

The chat tool offers real-time communication in a more simplistic manner. You can use chat to engage in conversation with all students, small groups of students, or individual students. Chat allows you to enter text that users can view in real time. Good opportunities for using the chat tool include question-and-answer sessions and group assignments.

All of these LMS tools encourage active engagement in learning. Keep in mind that a course environment where students feel valued for their experiences and their individual contributions increases motivation and retention.

Assignments

An LMS helps students complete and submit their work and instructors to review and process the work submitted. Students can upload their assignment files directly in the LMS, and instructors can download or view students' submissions and provide feedback and grades to each student. The assignment component of an LMS allows instructors to collect and organize all documents that students submit. Grading in an LMS can include pass/fail, point values, letter grades, and check marks for completion. Instructors also can return assignments to students for resubmission if necessary.

Instructors must create systems that ensure all students participate. An LMS offers instructors online assessment, automatic grading, organization of project work, and tracking of both group and individual progress. Keep in mind that the LMS should help you facilitate your course and should not dictate the direction of the course or inhibit your instruction in any way. Compiling high-quality content, identifying the audience, and using the functionality of the LMS to suit the delivery format of your choice all contribute to the success of an online course.

Chapter 4:
Course Creation Software

Basic Tools for Course Creation

By Krystle Feathers

As you begin to write your online course, various tools can help you develop content and media pieces. Not all tools work equally well, though, so you must weigh the pros and cons of each one before deciding which tools to use.

If you decide to make your course text-based and rely on lengthy lectures, you can present your material in a few different ways. For example, you can use an LMS's WYSIWYG editor, which allows you to conveniently and quickly insert text directly into the course. Anyone who has administrative access to the course can edit the content from any computer with an Internet connection. Built-in WYSIWYG editors work well for posting short announcements, but they may not be the best option for posting lecture material, because problems with maintenance, backups, and portability may occur. Length also can be a problem.

If you want to post a 10-page lecture to a lesson, for example, you will need to break up the material, or chunk it, before you insert it into the course. With a WYSIWYG editor, you must create new pages for each section of the chunked content; therefore, each time you want to update the material on a given page, the updates must be done manually (in the WYSIWYG editor) at every point that the material appears in the course. As you can imagine, using a WYSIWYG editor makes it difficult to maintain a course. If you use a WYSIWYG editor, you also will have no record of the material you placed in the course if the server hosting the software fails or some other technical difficulty occurs. You could lose all or part of your course.

In addition to these issues, you should consider portability when you insert content into your course. Best practice calls for developing a course independent of a specific LMS. If you use the WYSIWYG editor in one LMS, the material may not transfer properly if you need to duplicate the course in a different LMS.

An alternative to a WYSIWYG editor for inserting lecture material is hypertext markup language (HTML). Even if you think you know nothing about HTML, you encounter it virtually every time you visit a website. If you present your content in HTML, you must build the material outside of the LMS, upload the material to the course portal, and then link the material within the course content outline. The creation of content in HTML allows you to easily edit and maintain records of your content; however, you still must chunk the material into sections. Students will read one HTML page and then continue on to the next one, and so on, instead of scrolling through one long page.

Those who have extensive knowledge of HTML can write HTML code with any plain text editor, such as Notepad (included with most versions of Microsoft Windows), or a basic word processor, such as Wordpad (included with some versions of Microsoft Windows but considered more advanced than Notepad). However, you do not need to know HTML coding to use HTML documents in your course. You can use software such as Adobe Dreamweaver and simply type text or add photos to your page and let the program translate the material into HTML code.

Dreamweaver provides three views for users as they create pages: code, design, and split. If you want to manually write the HTML, use code view. If you want to design the pages with a WYSIWYG editor, use design view. If you want to see the code and the design at the same time, choose split view, which shows the design at the bottom of the window and the corresponding code at the top of the window. Figure 1 shows Dreamweaver in split view; the arrows point to the location of the tabs for selecting the desired view.

Figure 1. Dreamweaver in split view.

If you like the idea of keeping records and maintaining your course content but also want to present your students with all the material at one time and avoid the chunking process, you can use a software program familiar to most people: Microsoft Word. The Word option also lets you present your online course content in several different ways. You can, for example, upload your Word documents to the LMS for students to download and read. Keep in mind, however, that some students may not have Word installed on their computers and may not be able to download the material. To circumvent this incompatibility problem, save your Word documents in Rich Text Format (.rtf). Even students who do not own a copy of Word can read .rtf documents.

You also can publish content from a Word document as a PDF file, which ensures that all students can open and view the document as you intended them to see it. This is the most common and easiest way of presenting written information. You upload and download PDF files to the LMS the same way as you do with Word documents. The creation of a PDF file from a Word document also guarantees that students cannot edit your document. To read PDF files, students only need a copy of Adobe Acrobat Reader. Most computers come with this software installed; however, any student who does not have the software can download it for free from Adobe.com.

As the course writer, you should consider presenting course content to students in ways other than just plain text. A quality online course addresses multiple learning styles and includes interactive media pieces that engage students and help the instructor assess and reinforce comprehension.

Many instructors and course writers use Microsoft PowerPoint to present lecture material for their online courses. Breaking the content into smaller bulleted items helps to highlight key points; a corresponding script gives students additional information. Students can view the PowerPoint presentation and follow along with the script. You can enhance your PowerPoint presentations with audio versions of the script read aloud as students click on each slide; this option especially helps auditory learners connect with the information.

Although most educators agree that interactivity enhances knowledge retention, creating this type of media for the online environment can seem daunting. You may already have exercises prepared to supplement your face-to-face content but do not know how to translate that material into an online format. Several e-learning authoring tools have been created to help professionals use their time to develop content rather than learn complex programming languages. Articulate and SoftChalk are the two most popular tools in this category.

Articulate Global, Inc., the developer of the Articulate software, was founded in 2002, and the company now sells a wide variety of products, ranging from quiz makers to video encoders. Articulate's Presenter software offers users the ability to convert PowerPoint presentations to Flash-based presentations without having any Adobe Flash knowledge. One of Articulate's most well-known products, Engage, allows users to quickly and easily turn their content into interactive media pieces. With this software, you can create time lines, pyramids, glossaries, and process charts. You simply import your content into the software and arrange the material the way you want it. After you have created your interactive media piece, you can export it to various locations, including the Web, an LMS, or a CD. You can accomplish all of this without using multiple software programs or detailed Flash coding.

SoftChalk was also founded in 2002 and produces a similar product that allows you to create professional-looking courses without having much programming knowledge. Unlike Articulate, which focuses mainly on supplemental media objects, SoftChalk allows you to create entire courses—including text, graphics, and quizzes—all within one program. After you have developed your course, you can export it to HTML format, package individual lessons, or even publish to a specific LMS, such as Blackboard.

Developing an online course is a complex but rewarding process. Regardless of how much time, effort, and money you can devote to the process, you will find a wide range of options and tools, from basic to advanced, available to help you. Although programs such as Dreamweaver, Articulate, and SoftChalk can help you create engaging content and media, they also have their drawbacks. They are fee-based products that you must purchase and install before you can use them; therefore, you may want to experiment with course development before you make a major investment in supplemental software tools.

Thinking About the End User

By Krystle Feathers

The author of any online course must consider the student experience in the course design. Like face-to-face courses, online students have the opportunity to evaluate their courses when the term ends. Unlike face-to-face courses, however, most online courses do not feature synchronous sessions with instructor–student engagement. Instead, online students engage more with the content than with the instructor, which makes the content a necessary focal point for student satisfaction.

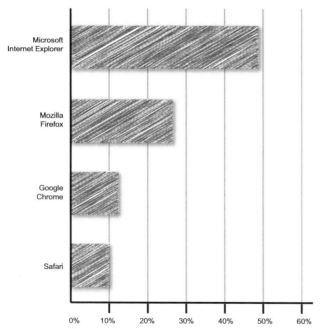

Figure 1. Percentage of users per browser in North America (StatCounter, 2011).

To ensure students' satisfaction, you must design your course for optimal Internet delivery. Although students demonstrate diverse technology skill sets and needs, solid preparation and planning can help you ensure that all students get the most out of your course.

As you develop your course, first consider your audience. For example, an online advanced computer course typically contains more technically skilled students than an English Composition I class does. As a result, the instructor of the advanced computer course can use more Internet jargon and even include more interactivity and social components. The students enrolled in the course are unlikely to need much direction on how to use the tools provided to them. In the English Composition I course, on the other hand, students may have fewer technology skills and, therefore, need more assistance using advanced technology products. As you design your course, identify the **minimum technology knowledge** your students must have to take the course. This step helps ensure that you address any gaps in technological knowledge that your students may have as you prepare the online course.

You also should consider the type of students enrolled in your course. Because adult students make up a large portion of the online course environment, make sure you consider the differences between adult learners and traditional college students. Adult learners are more problem-and-results-oriented as opposed to subject-future-oriented like traditional college students. Adult learners are self-directed and desire to learn and improve the skills that immediately impact their lives. In addition, they value participating in learning activities that enhance their knowledge. Adult learners typically have years of experience, are more likely than traditional college students to offer differing opinions, and need to see clear course expectations. Once you know what kinds of activities you need for your course, you can determine what technologies you will need to ensure that those activities can take place online.

Next, think about the types of media (e.g., videos, interactive elements, games) you will need for your course. The greater the variety of media you want to include, the more factors you must consider. While most computers purchased within the last 2 years have sufficient hardware capacity and the software needed to access an online course, not all students have the software installed to fully participate in the online course if you have not prepared the course materials for optimal Web delivery. To ensure that your course runs well for all students, you must deliver content using software that can run smoothly on the majority of operating systems and Web browsers.

Always use the most up-to-date and versatile software and regularly review your course content delivery methods in light of new technological trends, such as Internet browser upgrades. For example, Internet Explorer has led the browser market since Netscape Navigator was discontinued in 2008; however, other browsers have been introduced in the last few years, creating so-called browser wars. According to website analytics company StatCounter (2011), "Firefox overtook Microsoft's Internet Explorer (IE) to become the number one browser in Europe in December 2010." StatCounter (2011) further reports that "in December, Firefox took 38.11% of European market share, compared to IE's 37.52%" but that "in North America, IE still retains a clear lead in the browser market with 48.92% followed by Firefox (26.7%), Chrome (12.82%) and Safari (10.16%)." Based on these statistics, if you design an online course for only the dominant browser, half the students may have a poorer experience than they could have had with an optimal browser.

In addition to considering browsers, you must consider the user's Internet connection speed. For example, if you decide to incorporate video segments into your course, remember that download

MINIMUM TECHNOLOGY KNOWLEDGE
Computer skills that students must have to take a course.

speeds vary depending on each user's computer and Internet connection. Therefore, you should keep each segment short and to the point.

Further, you must consider the software needed for interactive course elements, such as flash cards. If you plan to include interactive multimedia pieces that reinforce learning, keep in mind that students may need to download additional software to play the media files.

Finally, you must consider how students will primarily view the course. Some mobile devices, such as iPads and iPhones, do not support Adobe Flash, one of the most common pieces of software used on standard websites. You will need to present this material in alternate formats for those mobile users.

As you can see, many aspects of the user experience deserve consideration as you develop your online course. Thinking about these issues before you design your course will help you provide your students with a positive learning experience. Proper planning will also save you development time because you will not have to make drastic changes after the course launches.

References
StatCounter. (2011). *Firefox overtakes Internet Explorer in Europe in browser wars*. Retrieved January 11, 2011, from http://gs.statcounter.com/press/firefox-overtakes-internet-explorer-in-europe-in-browser-wars

SECTION III

COMMON COMPONENTS OF AN ONLINE COURSE

Chapter 5:
Syllabus: Blueprint of a Course

INSTRUCTOR INFORMATION
Element of a syllabus that includes the instructor's name, email address, phone number, and office hours.

COURSE DESCRIPTION
Element of a syllabus that contains a brief summary statement or paragraph about the nature of the course and which matches the course description in the institution's catalog.

COURSE OBJECTIVES
Elements of a syllabus that detail the specific, measurable, clear, and related goals of the course as they pertain to student performance; also referred to as course outcomes.

Converting Face-to-Face Course Syllabi for Use in Online Courses

By Victoria Alexander

Converting a syllabus designed for a face-to-face course into one used for a fully online course entails less work than you may think. Face-to-face courses and their online counterparts usually have the same basic components: student participation, group exercises, individual exercises, and assessments. The real work in syllabus conversion involves designing alternative activities (or modifying existing ones) so that instructors can equitably assess students in a way that is consistent with the chosen course delivery method.

Standard Syllabi Components

Both face-to-face and online syllabi should include the following sections: instructor information, course description, course objectives (or course outcomes), course methodology, grading criteria, grade computation, and course policies. In addition, the syllabi for both face-to-face and online versions of the same class should provide identical course descriptions and course objectives because most accrediting bodies (especially regional ones) require that all sections of a course, regardless of the delivery method, assess students equally. The most significant differences between the two types of syllabi typically appear in the course methodology, grading criteria, and course policies. The remainder of this article breaks down the components of the syllabus and identifies the similarities and differences.

Instructor Information

Regardless of whether you teach an online class or a face-to-face class, you should make your contact information readily available on your syllabus. All syllabi should include **instructor information**, such as the instructor's name, email address, phone number, and office hours. The relevance of other contact information depends on the type of class. For example, if you teach a face-to-face course, you should include your office location; if you teach an online course, you should tell students how they can reach you. In a face-to-face course, you generally can expect that students will discuss matters with you before class, after class, or at your office during office hours. In an online course, however, synchronous sessions with students do not provide sufficient privacy for personal student discussions before or after the session. Online students also may not live close enough to travel to your office or be available to meet during your traditional office hours. For an online course, therefore, you must change how and when you are available.

To provide sufficient individual consultation, you should make yourself available electronically and by telephone. Chat sessions are the best electronic option because they allow for real-time communication as opposed to the asynchronous communication of email. Some learning management systems (LMSs) offer private chat rooms for meetings between the instructor and individual students. If you have that option, you should list "private chat room" as the location where students can reach you. If you do not have that option, ask your LMS administrator or a member of your institution's technology team what functionality exists on your LMS to provide private student consultations. If you do not have an LMS administrator or a technology team, you should notify students that you can consult with them on the phone or on campus. Ideally, you should provide at least two phone numbers: your office phone number and your mobile or home phone number. If you do not want to give your personal phone numbers, consider forwarding your office phone to your mobile phone or home phone during evening hours.

Course Description
A **course description** is a brief summary statement or paragraph about the nature of a course. Well-written course descriptions use active voice, whole sentences, and direct statements. To ensure consistency across sections and instructors, all instructors should take course descriptions directly from their institution's catalog.

Course Objectives (Course Outcomes)
Course objectives, or outcomes, detail the specific goals of the course as they relate to student performance. Strong course objectives are specific, measurable, clear, and related (Johnson, 2007). To be specific, objectives must identify the information students will learn in the class. To be measurable, objectives must identify the performance that students must demonstrate for mastery. To be clear, objectives must articulate the sum of knowledge addressed in the course. Finally, to be related, objectives must logically coexist, building on one another and/or complementing each other. The following table gives examples of weak and strong course objectives:

COMMON COMPONENTS OF AN ONLINE COURSE

WESTERN CIVILIZATION II COURSE OBJECTIVES (TRUNCATED)	
EXAMPLES OF WEAK COURSE OBJECTIVES	**EXAMPLES OF STRONG COURSE OBJECTIVES**
Understand major issues and differences in Western civilizations.	Summarize the political, social, and cultural perspectives of Western civilization.
Define colonization, and explain why it happened.	Review the significance of Western exploration and colonization.
Discuss major revolutions.	Critique the ideologies and impact of the Age of Reason, the Scientific Revolution, and the Cultural Revolution.
List the dates of World War I and World War II.	Describe the causes and significance of the Great Wars.

Since curriculum standardization has become a central theme in academia, you may find that objectives for your course already exist, having been established as part of the program's development. However, you still should review and update your course objectives to be sure they meet the four standards of good course objectives.

Course Methodology

Course methodology refers to how the class approaches student learning. Many online courses feature a variety of learning methods, including readings, case studies, tests, quizzes, and discussions. Describing the course methodology gives students some expectation of the materials they will use to learn in the class. It also gives students the information they need to determine how well-suited they are for the course.

For example, suppose a Western Civilization II course taught fully online states the following about its course methodology:

> *This course incorporates the use of a textbook, article readings, films, discussion forums, and timed examinations to facilitate and assess learning.*

From just that one sentence, students know that they will have to read a textbook and articles, watch films, discuss material with their classmates, and take timed exams. Students who have reading difficulties and students who do better with written essays than timed exams may elect not to take the course after discovering how the instructor expects them to learn in the class. The course methodology arms students with clear expectations of what they will do in the course.

Grading Criteria

Many students focus their attention on the section of the syllabus that lists the **grading criteria**. Adult students especially value having clear guidelines they can follow as they complete their coursework. Therefore, you should spend time writing unambiguous grading criteria for each method you will use to grade students. Well-written criteria address the most common questions related to course assessments. The following table highlights the differences between poorly defined criteria and precise criteria:

GRADING AREA	POORLY DEFINED GRADING CRITERIA	PRECISE GRADING CRITERIA
Discussion Forums	Students will respond to a discussion thread each week.	Each weekly lesson includes a discussion forum with one or more questions. Students are expected to address each question with thoughtful responses (approximately 150 words) that incorporate elements from the lesson's assigned readings. Students also must respond to at least one classmate's post (approximately 75 words) with meaningful feedback. Initial responses are due by Friday at 11:55 p.m. each week. Responses to classmates' posts are due by Sunday at 11:55 p.m. each week. Students can earn a maximum of 10 points each week at the instructor's discretion.
Papers	Students are responsible for submitting all assigned papers on time. Papers must be 2 to 3 pages long and demonstrate that students have thoroughly read the material.	This class requires students to write two papers. The first paper is due during lesson 4, and the second paper is due during lesson 8. Each paper must be at least 3 pages long, typed in Arial 11-point font, and single-spaced with 1-inch margins on all sides. Students can find the topics and deadlines for each paper listed in the course with the appropriate lesson. Late papers will not be accepted. Students must cite all references in APA format and include a references list, which is not included in the page count. Title pages are not accepted as a part of the page count. Well-written papers will address the topic thoroughly and include citations from the assigned readings and material from additional scholarly (i.e., researched) resources not assigned for the lesson.
Quizzes	Students will take a quiz each week.	Each lesson includes a short examination (i.e., quiz) that reviews the material covered in the lesson. The quizzes are timed and can only be taken once. Students must submit quizzes by Friday at 11:55 p.m. each week.

GRADING AREA	POORLY DEFINED GRADING CRITERIA	PRECISE GRADING CRITERIA
Exam	Students will take one comprehensive exam.	Lesson 8 includes a final exam for the whole course. The exam is comprehensive in nature and covers material from lessons 1 through 7. The exam is timed and randomized to ensure that each student receives a unique exam.

Grade Computation

The **grade computation** section of the syllabus is the second section to which students give considerable attention. You should specify the value of each graded item in the course so that students know how to weight their focus in the class. The following table shows a typical grade computation listed on a syllabus:

GRADING AREA	PERCENTAGE
Discussion Forums	20%
Papers	25%
Quizzes	20%
Exam	35%
TOTAL	**100%**

You can improve this section by detailing the value of each assignment, as shown in the following table:

GRADING AREA	NO. OF ITEMS IN COURSE	POINTS PER ITEM	TOTAL POINTS
Discussion Forums	8	10	80
Papers	2	50	100
Quizzes	8	10	80
Exam	1	140	140
		TOTAL	**400**

With the methodology shown, students can manage more carefully the amount of time they invest in graded items. For example, if confronted with the issue of focusing on discussion forum posts or writing a paper, students can easily gauge that each paper is worth five times the amount of a single discussion forum post and manage their time appropriately.

Course Policies

Many institutions use standardized syllabi with predefined **course policies**; however, instructors often must rewrite course policies designed for face-to-face courses to make them relevant for online courses. For example, attendance policies that discuss tardiness and use of cell phones do not apply to most online courses. If instructors do not consider student attendance when grading, then they can remove the attendance policy from the syllabus. However, if instructors do grade based partly on attendance, or if the institution requires all syllabi to include a policy on attendance, then online instructors should consider using an attendance policy similar to the following:

> **Attendance:**
> Students must access the online course regularly to ensure that they receive the most up-to-date announcements. The learning management system reports each participant's access times so that instructors can track student attendance. Students who access the course only one or two times per week may receive less consideration if they request extensions or make-up exams. It is in the best interest of each student to log in daily and actively participate in the course.

Other policies that instructors should review and update include, for example, make-up examinations, academic dishonesty, accommodations for students who have disabilities, and withdrawal from course enrollment.

Conclusion

Converting a face-to-face syllabus for use in an online course requires attention to detail and a clear determination of how the online course will work, including the learning management system's functionality and what the instructor expects students to do in the online course. The

COURSE POLICIES
Element of a syllabus that addresses attendance, make-up examinations, academic dishonesty, accommodations for students who have disabilities, and withdrawal from course enrollment.

syllabus sets the stage for course development and management. The construction of a well-defined online syllabus makes the development and management of an online course much easier.

References

Johnson, R. N. (2007). *Rubric for assessing course objectives*. University Park, PA: Penn State University. Retrieved December 20, 2010, from http://www.schreyerinstitute.psu.edu/pdf/Learning_outcomes_rubric.pdf

How to Write Measurable Objectives

By Victoria Alexander

Objectives play a fundamental role in designing appropriate instruction. Objectives enable instructors to (1) identify what students should know at the conclusion of an instructional activity, (2) organize instructional activities and materials, (3) determine assessment methods of student performance, and (4) create a level of accountability for student performance (Lasley, Matczynski, & Rowley, 2002). To successfully address these four components, the course writer or instructor must write the objectives in a measurable (but not overly prescriptive) manner. The best objectives, especially for online courses, provide enough information to measure student outcomes while also offering instructors sufficient freedom to adjust assessment methods according to the student population and the instructor's strengths. Measurable student objectives are **instructional objectives**, which Mager (1997) defined as "a collection of words and/or pictures and diagrams intended to let others know what you intend for your students to achieve" (p. 3). In other words, instructional objectives articulate what you consider satisfactory student performance.

Components of an Instructional Objective

According to Mager (1997), instructional objectives (1) state tangible outcomes, (2) relate to student performance, and (3) are specific. Tangible outcomes are easily measured and reflect an outwardly facing behavior. If you cannot see, feel, or hear the outcome, the outcome is not tangible. Two of the most commonly used words in objectives—*know* and *understand*—do not describe tangible outcomes. How do you see, feel, or hear someone knowing or someone understanding? Both words describe internalized cognitive processes. On the other hand, good instructional objectives require students to outwardly demonstrate competency.

In addition to stating tangible outcomes, instructional objectives should relate to student performance. At times, educational professionals confuse **instructional processes**, which are the methods used to deliver instruction, with student performance. For example, imagine that you teach an introductory counseling course. In preparing to teach the lesson on counseling multicultural families, you decide that a class discussion will help you more fully explore the topic. You determine that you can best lead that discussion by proposing alternative strategies for counseling multicultural families. As the instructor, your objective for the discussion is to propose alternative strategies for counseling multicultural families. However, your students' objective is to discuss the alternative strategies you propose rather than actually propose alternative strategies on their own. Instructional objectives reflect what students should do instead of the processes instructors employ to help students reach those objectives.

Third, instructional objectives are specific. For example, imagine that you teach a sociology course that requires students to name key sociologists of the 19th century by the end of the term. If you simply tell students that they must name sociologists, they may not produce the expected outcome. To ensure that students produce the expected outcome, you must clearly communicate that they must name 19th-century sociologists. Specific objectives minimize student confusion and enable you to create content and assessments that better serve those objectives.

Tips for Writing Measurable Objectives

1. *Refer to the Revised Bloom's Taxonomy for measurable verbs.*

   The **Revised Bloom's Taxonomy** classifies measurable verbs into hierarchical levels. Renowned educational psychologist Benjamin Bloom developed the original Bloom's Taxonomy in 1956. In 2001, a revised version was published, which clarified verb usage and reordered the top two levels. The Revised Bloom's Taxonomy chart, shown below, provides a small sample of the classification system:

REMEMBERING	UNDERSTANDING	APPLYING	ANALYZING	EVALUATING	CREATING
Define, identify, list, state, reproduce	Classify, indicate, match, select, summarize	Apply, examine, generalize, illustrate, record	Compare, contrast, differentiate, discriminate, examine	Argue, critique, defend, evaluate, judge	Construct, design, formulate, hypothesize, plan

2. *Build upon existing objectives.*

   If you are writing objectives for a course syllabus, first review the objectives for the program to which the syllabus belongs. Likewise, if you are writing objectives for a lesson, first review the objectives for the course. In either case, rewrite any objectives that do not meet the criteria of an instructional objective. Doing so enables you to create more appropriate instructional objectives.

3. *Break down larger or higher-order objectives into smaller objectives.*

Break down any existing objectives that have a large scope or require higher-order thinking skills (e.g., hypothesizing) into smaller, more manageable **subobjectives**. Breaking the objectives down helps you organize and group information for students. It also facilitates smooth content development. The following example illustrates the process of breaking down objectives:

Objective: Compare and contrast the constructivist view of education with the behaviorist view of education.
Subobjectives:
- *Define constructivism and behaviorism.*
- *Summarize the development of constructivism and behaviorism philosophies.*
- *Identify key constructivist theorists and behaviorist theorists.*
- *Describe the constructivist and behaviorist approaches to education.*

Review

Creating measurable objectives is an important part of designing successful online courses. Remember that these objectives communicate your expectations to students and help you prepare the most appropriate instructional materials. If you take the time to create measurable objectives, you can reduce the stress of course development.

References

Lasley, T. J., Matczynski, T. J., & Rowley, J. B. (2002). *Instructional models: Strategies for teaching in a diverse society* (2nd ed.). Belmont, CA: Wadsworth/Thomson Learning.

Mager, R. F. (1997). *Preparing instructional objectives: A critical tool in the development of effective instruction* (3rd ed.). Atlanta, GA: Center for Effective Performance.

Mapping Course Creation With the Syllabus

By Claudia Olea

When creating an online course, you should begin with a syllabus designed for online instruction. The syllabus serves as the blueprint for course development. The most important syllabus components for **course mapping** include measurable course objectives, required course materials, methods of instruction, and grading criteria. The objectives serve as a starting point for identifying course topics; the required course materials provide a baseline for thinking about necessary student resources; the course methodology provides guidance regarding the types of content you may use; and the grading criteria identify the learning activities you must include. All of these components work together to create a road map for course creation that will culminate in a course outline.

Step 1: Create topics from objectives.

When creating your course outline, first identify the major topics your measurable objectives address. For example, an introductory course on American government may have the following course objectives:

1. Analyze the framework of the constitutional foundation of the United States government, including the separation of powers, the federal structure, civil liberties, and civil rights.
2. Explain the importance and influence of the activities of individual citizens, interest groups, political parties, political processes, campaigns, elections, and the media regarding national government concerns and issues.
3. Describe the role and function of policy-making institutions of the national government, including Congress, the presidency, the judicial system, and the bureaucracy.

Possible topics based on these objectives include the following:

- Bureaucracy
- Campaigns
- Civil liberties
- Civil rights
- Congress
- Constitution
- Elections
- Federal structure
- Individual citizens
- Interest groups
- Judicial system
- Media
- Political parties
- President
- Separation of powers

Next, organize the topics. You can do this in different ways, depending on the nature of the course. For example, you may organize a history course by time period and a sociology course by themes or concepts. The topics identified can help you decide which approach to take. In the case of the introductory American government course, a themed approach is more logical than a time-oriented approach. One way to organize a course by themes involves grouping similar topics. The following table illustrates how to do this:

THEME	TOPICS
Concepts	Civil liberties, civil rights, constitution, federal structure, separation of powers
Government organization	Bureaucracy, Congress, president, judicial system
Nongovernmental influences	Interest groups, media
Voting	Campaigns, elections, individual citizens, political parties

Step 2: Break down objectives into subobjectives.

After you have organized your topics, return to the course objectives and break down each objective into smaller objectives, called subobjectives. To do this, ask yourself, "What do students need to know before they can achieve this objective?" For example, you can divide the course objective "Analyze the framework of the constitutional foundation of the United States' national government, including the separation of powers, the federal structure, civil liberties, and civil rights" into the following subobjectives:

- Define constitution, separation of powers, civil liberties, and civil rights.
- Outline the framework of the U.S. Constitution.
- Explain the concept of separation of powers.
- Review the federal structure.
- Differentiate between civil liberties and civil rights.
- List civil liberties provided by the U.S. Constitution.
- Explain how civil rights and civil liberties have developed over time.

The subobjectives determine what you will teach (i.e., instructional processes) and what you will assess (i.e., instructional objectives). Although not all subobjectives will lead to assessment, you should address all of them in the instructional process.

COURSE MAPPING
Using the syllabus as a blueprint for developing course topics, resources, content, and activities.

INSTRUCTIONAL VALUE
The measure of how important different pieces of content are to students in grasping course objectives or subobjectives.

Step 3: Align subobjectives with topics.

To ensure that your course flows well, you should create a table that matches each subobjective with the topic or topics it covers. The following table serves as an example. Note that some subobjectives can address multiple topics. In those instances, you should list the subobjective next to each topic it addresses so that you can see all the topics to which it applies. This table serves as the beginning of the course map.

CATEGORY	TOPIC	SUBOBJECTIVE
Concepts	Civil liberties	• Define constitution, separation of powers, civil liberties, and civil rights. • List the civil liberties provided by the U.S. Constitution.
	Civil rights	• Define constitution, separation of powers, civil liberties, and civil rights. • Differentiate between civil liberties and civil rights. • Explain how civil rights and civil liberties have developed over time.
	Constitution	• Define constitution, separation of powers, civil liberties, and civil rights. • Outline the framework of the U.S. Constitution.
	Federal structure	• Define constitution, separation of powers, civil liberties, and civil rights. • Review the federal structure.
	Separation of powers	• Define constitution, separation of powers, civil liberties, and civil rights. • Explain the concept of separation of powers.

Step 4: Classify subobjectives.

After beginning a map of categories, topics, and subobjectives, you should classify each subobjective as an instructional process, an instructional objective, or both. The subobjectives classified as instructional processes help you create instructional materials, while the subobjectives classified as instructional objects help you create lesson objectives and assessments. To categorize subobjectives properly, ask yourself, "What is the **instructional value** of this subobjective?" Subobjectives describing information that students must grasp before they can advance their knowledge in the course should take priority over other subobjectives. Subobjectives describing information that students could easily look up or quickly review may have less value.

For example, the subobjective "Define constitution, separation of powers, civil liberties, and civil rights" has significant instructional value because the course content uses the terms from the subobjective repeatedly throughout the course. On the other hand, the subobjective "List civil liberties provided by the U.S. Constitution" has less significant value because students can easily look up or reference the information. The latter subobjective would have a higher value in a course focused on civil rights guaranteed by the U.S. Constitution.

You should classify subobjectives with high value as instructional processes and instructional objectives. Conversely, you should classify subobjectives of mid- to low-value as instructional processes. The following table shows an example of these classifications:

SUBOBJECTIVE	TYPE
Define constitution, separation of powers, civil liberties, and civil rights.	Instructional process and instructional objective
Outline the framework of the U.S. Constitution.	Instructional process
Explain the concept of separation of powers.	Instructional process and instructional objective
Review the federal structure.	Instructional process and instructional objective
Differentiate between civil liberties and civil rights.	Instructional process and instructional objective
List civil liberties provided by the U.S. Constitution.	Instructional process
Explain how civil rights and civil liberties have developed over time.	Instructional process

After you have classified the subobjectives, you should map them to the course methodology and then to the required course materials.

Step 5: Map the course methodology to the subobjectives.

The course methodology communicates how students will learn. Many online courses feature written text, discussion forums, exams, and papers as part of their methodology. Because

ASSESSMENT TOOLS
Methods instructors use to satisfy instructional objectives (e.g., discussion forums, essays, and exams).

TEACHING METHODS
Methods instructors use to advance instructional processes (e.g., readings and video materials).

COURSE ROAD MAP
A table that identifies each lesson and states each lesson's objectives and activities that an instructor must develop for the course.

learning is an active process, it occurs through both teaching and assessment (when assessment includes feedback). To map subobjectives to the course methodology, review the syllabus, and list the methods used.

Continuing with the introductory American government course example, the syllabus lists the course methodology as the following:

This course provides instruction through the use of audiovisual materials, discussion forums, lectures, projects, quizzes, readings, and short essays.

Therefore, the course uses the following methods of instruction:
- *Audiovisual materials*
- *Discussion forums*
- *Lectures*
- *Projects*
- *Quizzes*
- *Readings*
- *Short essays*

Discussion forums, essays, and exams are all **assessment tools**; instructors should use them to satisfy instructional objectives. Readings and video materials are **teaching methods**; instructors should use them to advance instructional processes. To determine which methodology correlates with each subobjective, you must decide how best to provide instruction and/or assessment on the topic. The following questions can help bring the best methodology into focus:

1. Where does this objective fall in the Revised Bloom's Taxonomy?
2. What is the best way to present or assess this objective?

Take, for example, the subobjective "Define constitution, separation of powers, civil liberties, and civil rights." The Revised Bloom's Taxonomy lists the verb "define" in the remembering domain. At that level, memorizing information is important. Because students memorize text-based information the easiest, instructors should use the reading instruction method for teaching this subobjective. Additionally, given that definitions are either correct or incorrect (i.e., reason is not part of the memorization process), instructors should use exams to assess this subobjective.

The following table illustrates one way to map subobjectives to course methodology for the example introductory American government course:

SUBOBJECTIVE	TYPE	METHODOLOGY
Define constitution, separation of powers, civil liberties, and civil rights.	Instructional process and instructional objective	Reading, quiz
Outline the framework of the U.S. Constitution.	Instructional process	Reading
Explain the concept of separation of powers.	Instructional process and instructional objective	Reading, short essay
Review the federal structure.	Instructional process and instructional objective	Reading, quiz
Differentiate between civil liberties and civil rights.	Instructional process and instructional objective	Reading, discussion forum
List civil liberties provided by the U.S. Constitution.	Instructional process	Reading
Explain how civil rights and civil liberties have developed over time.	Instructional process	Audiovisual materials

Step 6: Map required course materials to subobjectives.

After you have mapped the subobjectives to the course methodology, you can look through your required course materials and identify which materials will give students the knowledge they need to fulfill the instructional process portion of your subobjectives. For example, students can fulfill many subobjectives by reading a required textbook or a print or Web-based article. One of the benefits of online courses is that their format allows you to link directly to information that students need to read. You may find that no existing materials succinctly address the subobjective. In that case, you should note those materials as not available or mark them for creation.

The following table shows one way to map subobjectives to required course materials for the introductory American government course:

SUBOBJECTIVE	INSTRUCTIONAL PROCESS METHODOLOGY	REQUIRED COURSE MATERIAL
Define constitution, separation of powers, civil liberties, and civil rights.	Reading	Handout
Outline the framework of the U.S. Constitution.	Reading	Handout
Explain the concept of separation of powers.	Reading	Lecture and/or online article
Review the federal structure.	Reading	Lecture and/or online article
Differentiate between civil liberties and civil rights.	Reading	Textbook
List civil liberties provided by the U.S. Constitution.	Reading	Lecture
Explain how civil rights and civil liberties have developed over time.	Audiovisual materials	Not available (to be created)

Step 7: Match the method of instruction to the grading criteria.

The next step in creating a course map involves matching the method of instruction to the grading criteria. In analyzing each subobjective individually, you may forget about the grading criteria you originally planned. If you reference your originally planned grading criteria on the table you created when determining the course methodology, you can easily see the correlation and modify the grading criteria or methodology as you deem fit. Remember that in an online course, you may rely more heavily on one type of grading criteria than another. For example, participation in discussions may not represent a significant portion of students' grades in a face-to-face course, but discussions may serve as the primary method of student assessment in an online course.

As an example, the following table shows the grading criteria for the example introductory American government course:

ASSESSMENT	GRADE (POINTS)
Discussion forums	20
Graded assignments	60
Essays	50

ASSESSMENT	GRADE (POINTS)
Quizzes	20
Project	50
Total	**200**

The table below shows one way to map the method of instruction to the grading criteria for the example introductory American government course:

SUBOBJECTIVE	INSTRUCTIONAL OBJECTIVE METHODOLOGY
Define constitution, separation of powers, civil liberties, and civil rights.	Quiz
Outline the framework of the U.S. Constitution.	N/A
Explain the concept of separation of powers.	Short essay
Review the federal structure.	Quiz
Differentiate between civil liberties and civil rights.	Discussion forum and project
List civil liberties provided by the U.S. Constitution.	N/A
Explain how civil rights and civil liberties have developed over time.	N/A

When mapping the method of instruction to the grading criteria, you must consider the parameters you set for the grading criteria. For example, in the table above, the subobjective "Differentiate between civil liberties and civil rights" has both discussion forum and project identified as the instructional objective methodologies. The discussion forum guidelines must lend themselves to encouraging discussion on that topic (e.g., requiring students to respond to each others' posts). Additionally, you should clearly define the project's guidelines and how the project relates to the course objectives. As you work through this portion of mapping, begin to brainstorm your grading criteria parameters.

Step 8: Create a course road map and content outline.
Now that you have finished mapping all aspects of the course objectives, subobjectives, and topics with the course methodology and grading criteria, you can create the overarching organizational tool for content.

A **course road map** is a table that identifies each lesson and states each lesson's objectives and activities. When you create a course road map, you create a tool for identifying all the parts and pieces you need to develop. As you do this, consider how the course will flow. You must make sure the course transitions smoothly between topics. You also should include for each lesson a brief lecture stating the objectives for that week and identifying the topics that the lesson's materials will cover.

For the introductory American government course, the following table illustrates a possible course road map for lesson 1:

LESSON 1: FOUNDATIONS OF AMERICAN GOVERNMENT	
Item	**Subobjectives to satisfy**
Lecture	• State the objectives for the lesson.
	• Identify topics discussed in the lesson's materials.
Reading	• Define constitution, separation of powers, civil liberties, and civil rights.
	• Outline the framework of the U.S. Constitution.
	• Explain the concept of separation of powers.
	• Review the federal structure.
	• Differentiate between civil liberties and civil rights.
	• List civil liberties provided by the U.S. Constitution.
Short essay	• Explain the concept of separation of powers.
Quiz	• Define constitution, separation of powers, civil liberties, and civil rights.
	• Review the federal structure.
Discussion forum	• Differentiate between civil liberties and civil rights.
Project	• Differentiate between civil liberties and civil rights.

After you have built the road map for each lesson, you can create the content outline that you will display on the syllabus for students to view. The content outline simply identifies the lessons for each week of the course.

For the example introductory American government course, the following table illustrates a possible course road map:

LESSON	TITLE
1	Foundations of American Government
2	Congress
3	The Presidency
4	The Judicial System
5	The Bureaucracy
6	The Election Process
7	Special Interest Groups
8	The Media

Summary

Creating a course road map is a process. You start with the course's global outcomes (i.e., course objectives) and drill down to the specific tasks that students must complete to demonstrate competency in the course. You then identify instructional processes that the course material must address to ensure successful student competency. Finally, you classify and organize your work into a road map for course development and a course outline.

Remember that a sound syllabus contains a course description; lists the required textbooks, institutional policies, course objectives, and grading criteria; and describes each lesson activity within the course and the grading criteria for those activities. A sound syllabus also includes a course outline, instructor policies, and instructor expectations. Since students who take online courses generally take them on their own terms and time schedules, they need syllabi that clearly tell them what to expect from their courses so that they do not have to contact their instructors for information unless they have additional questions regarding the course components. A sound syllabus creates the foundation for a sound course, especially if the course writer uses the syllabus to map the course development. Thus, the syllabus and the course should work together cohesively. Keeping in mind that you are the course writer first and the instructor second (if you will also teach it) should help you develop the course from the syllabus.

**Chapter 6:
Lessons: Course Content**

SUBJECT MATTER EXPERT (SME)
Someone who is an expert in a particular field.

MODULAR CONTENT
Collection of learning resources developed as a single learning object.

LEARNING RESOURCES
Instructional materials designed to confer knowledge and that are typically used in an online course as an equivalent replacement for face-to-face lectures.

Developing Modular Content
By Victoria Alexander

When developing an online course, course authors should consider who will use the course. Often, one **subject matter expert (SME)** creates online courses, but then several SMEs instruct them over time. Because online courses may have multiple instructors and require updates and changes over time, designing courses as modular provides sufficient flexibility to ensure that instructors can adapt courses to their teaching style and update the content without needing to rewrite the entire course.

Modular content refers to a collection of **learning resources** developed as a single learning object. Each learning object functions like a building block—independent and self-contained but capable of being paired with other building blocks. When a course author builds an online course using a collection of learning objects, this course has a **modular course design**.

How to Develop Modular Content
Four steps exist in the creation of modular content. First, you have to set the objective. Remember, modular content acts as a building block. It is a single learning object used for a specific purpose. The objective for modular content specifies how to use it. Without an objective, you cannot successfully develop learning resources for the learning object.

Second, you have to decide the best way to address the objective. One way to determine the best approach is to decide what skill students need to demonstrate competency of the objective. Consider the objective "Define instruction." Should students see the term and definition in writing? Should they hear the term and definition spoken out loud? Should they see a video about the term and definition? Defining a word requires a very low-level cognitive skill (memory recall). Students should be able to recall information fairly easily. Given the low skill needed, using text may be the best approach for addressing that objective.

Now consider the objective "Illustrate the process of instruction." To illustrate a process requires a higher level of cognitive skill. To successfully meet this objective, students must know the instruction, understand it, apply it, and analyze it. Addressing this objective, therefore, may require content that has more depth and visuals than text alone can provide. As such, you may need text with graphics, audio, or video.

Third, you have to create content that meets **scholarly publishing standards**. Published scholarly works are unbiased, communicate clearly, and contain proper formatting. In the case of text-based materials, professionals should edit, proofread, and design the content in an appropriate layout. Audio-based materials should feature excellent sound quality (devoid of air and inappropriate background noise). Audio-visual presentations should feature excellent sound quality and appropriate visuals to reflect the spoken content. Creating content that does not meet scholarly publishing standards may reduce a learning object's compatibility with other learning objects. Great differences in the quality level of learning objects can create an overall negative course experience for students.

Finally, you must remain focused on the objective. For a learning object to be reusable with other learning objects, it cannot inadvertently address objectives for other learning objects. For example, revisit the objective "Illustrate the process of instruction." To meet this learning objective, students must know the definition of instruction; however, the learning object that addresses the objective "Illustrate the process of instruction" should not define instruction. Remember, learning objects must be self-contained so course authors can pair them with other learning objects. If the learning object that addresses the objective "Illustrate the process of instruction" also meets the objective "Define instruction," course authors cannot easily couple this learning object with another learning object that defines instruction. The two learning objects may define instruction differently and thus create a confusing learning experience for students. To be certain that your learning objects work together and are reusable with other learning objects, each learning object must only address the specific objective you intended to address. You can always create additional objectives and learning objects to address content your current learning object does not cover.

References

Advanced Distributive Learning. (2008, July 31). *ADL guidelines for creating reusable content with SCORM 2004*. Retrieved from http://www.adlnet.gov/wp-content/uploads/2011/07/ADL_ Guidelines_Creating_Reusable_Content.pdf

MODULAR COURSE DESIGN
An online course built using a collection of learning objects.

SCHOLARLY PUBLISHING STANDARDS
Stipulations that require published scholarly works to communicate clearly and to be unbiased and formatted properly.

DIRECT INSTRUCTION
Teaching method in which the instructor delivers information and outlines directions for attaining certain competencies; most commonly used instructional strategy.

INDIRECT INSTRUCTION
Teaching method that focuses on student involvement and problem solving and for which the instructor has more of a facilitator role.

INTERACTIVE INSTRUCTION
Environment of discussion and sharing between the instructor and students as well as among individual students.

Instructional Content Delivery Formats

By Claudia Olea

Instructional content substantially affects the quality of online courses. In a world revolutionized by the Internet's ability to provide instant access to information, instructional content has become education's vehicle for delivering quality asynchronous education. For most course writers, designing and organizing content requires considerable time, planning, and research. Unfortunately, course writers often make format decisions based on their own convenience rather than on the best instructional strategy for the course, which leads to incorrect use of text, audio, and video formats for instructional content.

In addition to the delivery format for instructional content, relevant considerations for course design include the optimal instructional strategy, the subject matter, the end users, and the timeline for course development.

Instructional Strategy Considerations

An instructional strategy is a method used to deliver instruction. Education professionals often group instructional strategies into five categories: direct instruction, indirect instruction, interactive instruction, independent study, and experiential instruction.

Direct Instruction

Direct instruction is the most commonly used instructional strategy because it allows instructors to effectively deliver information and outline directions for attaining certain competencies. It is also the most instructor-led model of the five instructional strategies. The model includes five phases: orientation, presentation, structured practice, guided practice, and independent practice. The instructor does most of the leading in the first three phases and less in the last two phases (Joyce, Weil, & Calhoun, 2004). Direct instruction includes, for example, structured overviews, lectures, explicit teaching, drills and practice, comparisons and contrasts, didactic questions, and demonstrations (Saskatoon Public Schools, 2009).

Indirect Instruction

Indirect instruction requires more student involvement related to problem solving and curiosity, and the instructor's role shifts to that of a facilitator. Indirect instruction includes, for example, problem solving, case studies, reading for meaning, inquiry, reflective discussion, writing to inform, concept formation, concept mapping, and concept attainment (Saskatoon Public Schools, 2009).

Interactive Instruction

With **interactive instruction**, students learn through a well-constructed environment of discussion and sharing between the instructor and the students as well as among individual students. Interactive instruction includes, for example, debates; role-playing; panels; brainstorming; discussions; laboratory groups; think, pair, and share; cooperative learning; problem solving; structured controversy; tutorial groups; interviewing; and conferencing (Saskatoon Public Schools, 2009).

Independent Study

With **independent study**, the instructor encourages student ingenuity through self-study or study within small groups. Independent study includes, for example, essays, computer-assisted instruction, journals, learning logs, reports, learning activity packages, correspondence lessons, learning contracts, homework, research projects, assigned questions, and learning centers (Saskatoon Public Schools, 2009).

Experiential Instruction

Experiential instruction focuses on the process of learning rather than on the result of learning. Instructors make the student learning environment inductive, activity-oriented, and learner-centered. Experiential instruction includes, for example, field trips, narratives, conducting experiments, simulations, games, storytelling, focused imaging, field observations, role-playing, model building, and surveys (Saskatoon Public Schools, 2009).

After you have determined the appropriate instructional strategy, you can determine the appropriate instructional format. For example, suppose you must teach the law of supply and demand. Students may learn about this topic in a variety of ways, including reading, listening, and observing the concept in practice. Given that supply and demand is a fundamental concept used

INDEPENDENT STUDY
Self-study or study within small groups.

EXPERIENTAL INSTRUCTION
Teaching method that focuses on the process of learning rather than the result of learning; characterized by an inductive, activity-oriented, learner-centered learning environment.

to explain the more complex workings of economics, you may determine that students should not only read about the concept, but also see it used in everyday life. When you consider the need for students to read about and observe supply and demand, you can begin to envision using text and visually based content items to deliver that instruction.

Subject Matter Considerations

You also can determine your instructional format based on the subject matter. Some subject matters lend themselves well to text, while others require more interactive media. For example, a literature course that reviews 20th-century poets typically includes a large collection of readings, whereas a course on film studies is likely to incorporate a large collection of videos. If you consider the subject matter for your course, you can easily identify which format is more appropriate for the content.

End-User Considerations

Students are the end users of online courses. Each student has specific learning needs and equipment requirements they must meet before they can access an online course. Designing course materials that account for those needs and the available technology will greatly improve each student's learning experience. For example, if you are creating a reading course designed for remedial students, you should consider delivering content through multiple instructional strategies so that students have diverse pathways to learning. Additionally, if you are creating a personal finance course designed for young adults entering college, you should consider incorporating interactive and experiential strategies because that age group may have interactive expectations and needs.

Timeline Considerations

Time is a large factor in course creation. The more complex the instructional strategy, the more time you will need to create the instructional content. You can quickly determine how much time you need to create a course if you calculate how much time you typically need to teach the course and then double that number. For example, if a three-credit-hour course typically requires 45 hours of in-class time, then you will need approximately 90 hours to create the course. That time includes planning the course, designing the instructional content, building the course in the learning management system (LMS), and preparing the parameters of the course (e.g., grade book, due dates, and times to release content). If you do not have enough time to accomplish all these tasks, focus your time on creating assessments and then look for resources to provide instructional content.

Choosing the Format

When it comes to placing content on the learning management system, a variety of formats exist for content placement. The most common formats are text, audio, and video. Some courses have only one of each format for all the content, some have two out of the three types, and some have all the different formats. The type of format the content will be placed in usually depends on the instructor's vision of the course, the instructor's teaching style, the subject matter, resources for course development that are available to the instructor, the timeline for course development, and the best format for the end users, or the students, which will enable them to have a great learning experience.

Text

Text is the most common format used to deliver instructional content. Learning management systems come with text editors that provide basic formatting similar to what Microsoft Word offers. One benefit of text is its versatility. You can read it, turn it into audio (with a text-to-speech reader), and make it portable (through printing). Another benefit of text is that you can easily change it. If you publish text directly inside an LMS, you can change the text whenever you need to do so. If you convert the text into a noneditable document (e.g., a secure PDF file), you can still update it easily—but so can anyone else who has the original file from which you constructed the PDF. The versatile and adaptable nature of text makes it a good choice for delivering instructional content that requires memorization or frequent updates. Some examples of instructional content best suited for text include definitions, poems, and data. One drawback of using text is that it lacks interactivity. Also, online learners who do not read well may struggle with a course that uses text as its sole or primary format for delivering instructional content.

When writing text-based instructional content, you should consider how people may use the content and then select the appropriate voice. For example, if you are writing a course that other instructors may teach, use the third-person point of view. Use of first or second person voice implies that the instructor is the writer, which is not appropriate for courses that other instructors teach or courses that include multiple viewpoints. If you are writing instructions or tutorials, however, you should use the second-person point of view.

Additionally, you should consider the purpose of the work. For example, if you are teaching a course on current trends in health care, make sure you substantiate any claims with references because your discussions will likely cover recent research not yet considered common knowledge. Introductory courses, on the other hand, may require fewer references, as they tend to include more commonly accepted information.

Finally, do not forget to ask someone else to read your work for clarity. Even the best writers can benefit from a third-party reading. Often, word processors do not catch incorrect word usage or unclear sentences.

Audio

Audio is the next most commonly used content delivery format. Many instructors choose audio as a way to provide lectures (i.e., a method of direct instruction).

You can determine whether audio will work as the best content delivery format for your lectures if you consider the subject matter of the course. For example, language courses benefit from audio lectures because students need to know how languages sound phonetically as well as how they are written. However, providing an audio lecture for a business writing course would not benefit students if the instructor was outlining how to write a business proposal.

Although instructors do need to think about how they provide their lectures for face-to-face classrooms as they plan for online delivery, instructors should never record their in-class lectures. Also, to ensure compliance with the federal Americans with Disabilities Act (ADA), instructors must make sure they provide scripts along with their audio lectures. Typically, audio lectures work best when published in .mp3 format because that format provides excellent device compatibility.

Video

Video lectures also have become popular for delivering instructional content. Just as you must consider the subject matter of the course when deciding whether to use audio for lectures, you also must consider the subject matter when deciding whether to use video for lectures. For example, in a forensic science class, video would benefit students because the subject matter expert in the video could demonstrate real-life procedures in processing a crime scene that he or she could not explain using audio alone. However, a video recording of an instructor lecturing about different law enforcement agencies in the United States would not benefit students in a criminal justice course. As with audio lectures, instructors should never video record in-class lectures. Instructors also must make sure to provide scripts along with video lectures to ensure ADA compliance. The best formats for publishing video are .mp4 and .mpeg.

Summary

When contemplating the optimal content delivery format for your students, keep in mind that students may need to purchase or download resources to access the content. You should also consider the issues of student learning styles and disabilities. Some students learn better through visual means, while others learn better through auditory means, and still others learn better through both visual and audio means. Also consider that most students choose to take online courses because they appreciate the asynchronous experience that online education allows them. As you choose the content delivery format you will use to develop your course, make sure you take into account the asynchronous quality of online courses, the students' different learning styles, and the possible disabilities the students may bring to the course.

References

Joyce, B. R., Weil, M., & Calhoun, E. (2004). *Models of teaching* (7th ed.). Boston: Pearson Education.

Saskatoon Public Schools. (2009). *Instructional strategies online*. Retrieved February 17, 2011, from http://olc.spsd.sk.ca/de/pd/instr/index.html

Course Resources
By Joe Mochnick

You can enhance your course and engage online students if you include course resources, practice activities, and supplemental materials in every lesson. You can use a variety of resources in your course as long as you remember the purpose of these resources: to enhance student learning through additional content. **Course resources** give students the opportunity to explore subject matter outside of written lectures, assignments, and activities. While lectures and activities deliver the content, course resources reinforce learning. Constructivist theorists, such as Jean Piaget, proposed that through a process called "**scaffolding**," educators can provide students with a structure for learning that reinforces their existing knowledge and helps them explore new information through self-motivation. Correctly using resources in an online course can help you build a framework for successful learning and aid in student comprehension and retention in the online classroom.

Selecting the Right Resource
Choosing the right resource for your online course depends greatly on the content you have developed. The resources you select should be relevant and appropriate and provide the best opportunity to enhance student learning. Some common examples of course resources include: Internet resources, articles and supplementary readings, study guides, PowerPoint slides, glossaries, and flash cards.

Internet Resources
Linking to Internet sites promotes student learning outside the online classroom. When choosing Internet links, look for reputable and scholarly sites that provide credible information that reinforces what you have presented to the students. Some common sites, such as Wikipedia and About.com, contain a great deal of helpful information but usually do not meet the scholarly criterion, because anyone can create content for these sites and because the sites do not systematically perform diligent reviews. In addition to using reputable sites, make sure you point to specific resources rather than general sites. For example, in a course on American politics, you may want students to learn about the role of the president's press secretary. However, you may not want to point

students to the White House's home page, because it serves as a gateway to information—some of which is not relevant to the point you want to reinforce. Instead, you should point students to the Web page specific to the press secretary. Further, to ensure that students understand the purpose of the link, you should provide a brief description about the site. Finally, make sure you periodically check your course for broken links, as websites and addresses often move or change.

Articles and Supplementary Readings

Supplementary articles can significantly enhance your course and provide students with additional information outside textbook assignments and written lecture material. As with Internet resources, you should include only credible and scholarly journal articles, particularly those that have passed the peer-review process in which readers, editors, or scholars from the same field approve the article's content. If you do not know whether an article has been peer-reviewed, you may consult **Ulrich's Periodicals Directory**, a comprehensive and widely used database of scholarly journals and periodicals. **JSTOR** (Journal Storage) is another popular online resource for locating scholarly articles, and most university and college libraries are licensed to use it. Also, contact your institution's librarian about using resources available in the institution's electronic databases. Often, you can link directly to these resources within the course, which reduces the need for students to connect to external websites.

Study Guides

Many instructors use study guides to scaffold student learning and help students prepare for online assessments. Study guides may include chapter outlines; key terms and concepts; and visual diagrams, such as concept maps and charts. You also can summarize the main ideas of your lecture material in a format to which students can quickly refer when preparing for exams. Study guides help students organize, comprehend, and retain information. You can include study guides in every lesson you create.

PowerPoint Slides

If you want to add multimedia to your online classroom, PowerPoint presentations are an excellent alternative to written material, and you can easily create, host, and stream the slides online. If your online class uses a textbook, check to see if the publisher includes supplementary PowerPoint presentations that you can download for free from its companion website. You must remember, however, that publisher resources often are copyrighted and you must obtain the publisher's permission before you host copyrighted resources in your online classroom. Depending on which publishing company has produced your textbook, gaining permission is generally a quick and painless process that involves verifying the instructor's institutional and course information. If you do request permission to use copyrighted material, make the request early enough to allow at least a few weeks for the publishing company to process and grant your request. Most schools have a representative for each major publishing company.

Glossaries

Glossaries provide quick access to a collection of specialized terms and definitions that appear within your lesson and throughout your course. Adding a glossary to each of your lessons helps students become familiar with new or difficult terms and use them more easily in lessons and assessments. As you write your course, bold or highlight terms you want students to learn. By providing a short 5- to 10-word list at the end of each lecture, you can effectively enhance your lessons and promote memory retention in students.

Flash Cards

Flash cards help students drill and practice their knowledge of a given topic and reinforce key material from your lessons. They are also easy to add to online lessons. Flash cards work well for drilling students on vocabulary terms, formulas, facts, and lesson concepts. For flash cards to work effectively, they must relate to your topics and assessments and present a unique problem or question that tests students' knowledge. Flash cards can also help students identify their strengths and weaknesses related to particular topics, aid them in memorization, and help them prepare for exams.

Conclusion

In today's online classrooms, a wealth of resources is available to aid you in your course development; however, you must make sure you do not add course resources simply for the sake of adding resources. Course resources should add depth to your course and enhance or expand your lesson objectives and goals. Including resources gives online students the tools they need to further their knowledge on their own terms and puts them in control of their learning. You should not grade students on their use of these resources; rather, you should include the resources to encourage students to seek knowledge on an intrinsic level and gain new knowledge as a reward unto itself. When resources are relevant and reinforce learning, students have a better framework for successful learning and can engage more fully in your online classroom.

Chapter 7: Assignments:
Assessment of Course Comprehension

ONLINE COURSE ASSIGNMENTS
Assignments that are specific, flexible, and modular so they work well in an online course.

SPECIFIC ASSIGNMENTS
Assignments that require little to no additional direction from instructors.

Developing Assignments for Asynchronous Online Learning

By Victoria Alexander

One of the many challenges facing online course authors involves developing assignments that work well in an online course. Ideally, **online course assignments** are specific enough to ensure that students can complete them without additional instructor direction, flexible enough that they can work in any LMS, and modular enough that changes to other assignments will not affect them. Those specifications are no small order, which means online course authors must give almost as much consideration to constructing assignments as they do to creating the objectives on which they base the assignments. As you author online courses, taking the following steps can help ensure that you develop specific, flexible, and modular online course assignments.

Creating Specific Assignments

As an online course author, you should design **specific assignments** that allow students to complete the assignments with little to no additional direction. One benefit of online learning is that students are expected to be somewhat self-sufficient and do not require a lot of hand-holding. However, if you create vague assignments, students have to depend more on their instructors for clarity. To build on the existing expectation for online learners to be self-sufficient, you must design assignments that clearly communicate the instructor's expectations. The following chart presents some examples of assignments written with specificity sufficient for online learners to work independently:

	POORLY WRITTEN	WELL-WRITTEN	RATIONALE
READING ASSIGNMENT	Read chapter 5 of your textbook.	Read chapter 5 of Shah, A. J., & Dias, L. P. (2010). *Introduction to business*. New York: McGraw-Hill Higher Education.	The course may use multiple textbooks, and editions may change. Writing the reading assignment in citation style reduces the potential for error and confusion.

	POORLY WRITTEN	WELL-WRITTEN	RATIONALE
DISCUSSION ASSIGNMENT	What characteristics do you think make people successful entrepreneurs?	Using the guidelines for discussion forum postings (see syllabus for details), write a response to the following prompt. Then provide constructive feedback to the posts of at least two other classmates.	When completing an assignment, students should be aware of all expectations. You do not need to repeat the criteria in the assignment when you have already covered it in the syllabus. However, you should reference the criteria in the body of the assignment for reinforcement and clarity.
GRADED ASSIGNMENT	Complete the problems on pages 210 and 211.	Complete problems 1 through 4 on pages 211 and 212 of Shah, A. J., & Dias, L. P. (2010). *Introduction to business.* New York: McGraw-Hill Higher Education. Refer to the guidelines for graded assignments listed in the course syllabus.	Identifying the specific items students must complete and the tools they need to complete them ensures that students have all the information they need to work independently.

Creating Flexible Assignments

Well-written online courses can reuse **flexible assignments** for a number of years and across different platforms. Instructors can reuse authentic assessments in particular for several terms without needing to perform significant revision. In those years or terms, however, technology will most likely change. Additionally, colleges and universities may decide to adopt a different delivery system for online courses. To account for such changes, you must make sure your online assignments are flexible—that is, written to work in any learning management system. The following chart presents some examples of how you can write assignments to allow for flexibility:

FLEXIBLE ASSIGNMENTS
Assignments that instructors can reuse for a number of years and across different platforms without needing to perform significant revision.

MODULAR ASSIGNMENTS
Assignments that allow instructors to update, edit, change, or delete assignments without affecting other course materials and that do not reference materials in a manner that suggests their placement or order in a course.

	POORLY WRITTEN	WELL-WRITTEN	RATIONALE
READING ASSIGNMENT	Read the article for lesson 1 by clicking on the course home page and choosing the electronic reserve. You can then select the article labeled "Lesson 1 Reading."	Read the following article available on the electronic reserve: Glaeser, E. L., Kerr, W. R., & Ponzetto, G. A. M. (2010, January 1). Clusters of entrepreneurship. *Journal of Urban Economics, 48*(1), 150. *Note: If you need assistance locating articles on the electronic reserve, check the syllabus for assistance.*	The placement of materials often changes with technology upgrades and varies by LMS. By removing LMS-specific navigation directions from an assignment, you can reduce the potential for error when the technology changes.
DISCUSSION ASSIGNMENT	Answer the discussion question your instructor posted this week by clicking on "Add a New Discussion Topic."	Using the guidelines for discussion forum postings (see syllabus for details), write a response to the following question: *How has entrepreneurship changed over the past 50 years?*	How a feature works varies according to system and system version. Assignments should avoid including directions on how to use a feature so that instructors can reuse them over time and across systems with little to no modification.
GRADED ASSIGNMENT	Write a 2-page summary of the book Kiyosaki, R. T., & Lechter, S. L. (2000). *Rich dad, poor dad: What the rich teach their kids about money—that the poor and middle class do not!*. New York: Warner Business Books. Submit your paper via the drop box.	Submit a 2-page summary of the book Kiyosaki, R. T., & Lechter, S. L. (2000). *Rich dad, poor dad: What the rich teach their kids about money—that the poor and middle class do not!*. New York: Warner Business Books. Refer to the syllabus for guidelines.	Different systems and different system versions call features by different names. Terms such as "drop box" may not appear in every system. Avoiding LMS-specific functionality can help ensure assignments are flexible enough for use across different systems.

Creating Modular Assignments

Modular assignments allow instructors to update, edit, change, or delete assignments without affecting other course materials. For an assignment to be modular, it cannot reference materials in a manner that suggests their placement or order in a course. The following chart presents some examples of how you can write assignments for modularity:

	POORLY WRITTEN	WELL-WRITTEN	RATIONALE
READING ASSIGNMENT	Having read the lecture for lesson 2, read chapters 1 and 2 of Shah, A. J., & Dias, L. P. (2010). *Introduction to business*. New York: McGraw-Hill Higher Education.	Read chapters 1 and 2 of Shah, A. J., & Dias, L. P. (2010). *Introduction to business*. New York: McGraw-Hill Higher Education.	Instructors often change the order of lessons. To avoid confusing students, include in assignments only the information that students need to complete the assignments successfully.
DISCUSSION ASSIGNMENT	Having read the article for this week, answer the following question on the discussion forum: *The authors discuss barriers to action on improving C players. What other barriers do you see? Do you agree or disagree with the authors?*	After reading the following article, discuss what barriers you see to improving C players. Also, note if you agree or disagree with the authors. Axelrod, B., Handfield-Jones, H., & Michaels, E. (2002, January 1). A new game plan for C players. *Harvard Business Review, 80*(1), 80-88.	Instructors often change reading assignments as new material becomes available or original items become unavailable. By ensuring that students have all the information they need to complete an assignment within the assignment's body, you can minimize confusion.
GRADED ASSIGNMENT	Building on the business plan you started in week 2 of your course project, describe your service or product offerings in 1 to 2 pages.	Using the guidelines outlined in the syllabus for graded assignments, write a 1- to 2-page summary of the services or products you would offer as part of a business plan.	Instructors can potentially use assignments for a variety of purposes, and instructors often change their assignments as they deem appropriate. By keeping assignments focused on a particular task, you allow instructors to use each assignment as they deem appropriate for the courses.

Conclusion

Well-written online assignments function almost as an assignment bank. When they are specific, flexible, and modular, instructors can adopt them to use as they deem appropriate. Instructors can also reuse these assignments without much modification across systems and versions. Further, instructors can even use them across courses when subject matters correlate. The best strategy for developing assignments that are specific, flexible, and modular is to develop each assignment individually and align it with an objective. In doing so, you are more likely to create meaningful assignments that have a single focus.

Designing Assignments That Motivate Students

By Victoria Alexander

While online learning is often highlighted as the best instructional model for intrinsically motivated adult learners, course authors should recognize the importance of assignments in motivating students to complete a course. Especially in online courses, assignments can serve as a deciding factor between students persisting or "going dark" (i.e., students becoming disengaged and nonresponsive). To encourage course completion, course authors should create assignments that motivate students and foster student engagement in the course. One approach that instructional designers use to create motivating assignments is to craft assignments that meet the criteria for the **ARCS Model of Motivational Design**. ARCS is an acronym that stands for attention, relevance, confidence, and satisfaction. While the model, developed by instructional systems designer Dr. John Keller, is actually a methodology for designing instruction as a whole, some instructional designers have used it successfully for building specific online course assignments. By building on the model's premise that students must value the task and believe they can achieve it, course authors can develop meaningful assignments that encourage students to achieve academic success.

Attention

Assignments, by nature, are work. They are specific tasks students are required to complete as a part of the learning process. However, they do not have to come across as pure work. Almost any assignment can become interesting by addressing the attention aspect of the ARCS model.

The ARCS model gains students' **attention** using the following three strategies: capture interest, stimulate inquiry, and maintain attention. To capture interest, course authors should inject unexpected events or excitement into the instruction. To stimulate inquiry, course authors should appeal to students' curiosity. To maintain interest, course authors should vary the instructional aspects with relative consistency. The following are examples of each:
- *Capture interest:* A communications instructor uses a political cartoon to spur debate in a discussion forum.
- *Stimulate inquiry:* A logics instructor asks students to create a riddle for their classmates to solve as a means to demonstrate problem solving.

ARCS MODEL OF MOTIVATIONAL DESIGN
Instructional system for designing overall instruction or individual course assignments that emphasizes that students must value the task and believe they can achieve it.

ATTENTION
Aspect of the ARCS Model of Motivational Design that says assignments should capture students' interest, stimulate inquiry, and maintain students' attention.

RELEVANCE
Aspect of the ARCS Model of Motivational Design that says assignments should relate to students' goals, match their interests, and tie to their experiences.

CONFIDENCE
Aspect of the ARCS Model of Motivational Design that says assignments should set success expectations, success opportunities, and personal responsibility for students.

SATIFSACTION
Aspect of the ARCS Model of Motivational Design that says assignments should facilitate intrinsic satisfaction, rewarding outcomes, and fair treatment.

- *Maintain attention:* A sociology instructor switches the type of readings that students complete each week between research papers, short stories, blogs, and news articles.

Relevance

The **relevance** aspect of the ARCS model relates to connecting students with instruction. Course authors can achieve relevance in a variety of ways that reflect the following three strategies: relate to goals, match interests, and tie to experiences. To relate to goals, students should receive the specific purpose, or objective, of the assignment. To match interests, students should have the opportunity to deliver results according to their strengths or how they perform best. To tie to experiences, students should draw from models or their own experience. The following are example assignments of each category:

- *Relate to goals:* An English instructor begins a writing assignment with "Good essays require a thesis. In this assignment, you will construct a thesis…"
- *Match interests:* A psychology instructor allows students to present a biographical review of their preferred psychologist in any of the following ways: in writing, via a podcast, or using a video presentation.
- *Tie to experiences:* A business instructor directs students to identify the qualities of good customer service by describing their best and worst customer service experiences.

Confidence

The **confidence** aspect of the ARCS model relates to students feeling that they can succeed. Students arguably can attain success only when expectations of learning are clear. As such, Keller identified three strategies to build confidence in students: success expectations, success opportunities, and personal responsibility. Success expectations refer to the clear articulation of expectations through items such as standards, rubrics, and grading criteria. Success opportunities refer to diversified and interlinking activities that incrementally prepare students for performance achievement. Personal responsibility refers to students' ability to directly affect their success. The following are examples of each category:

- *Success expectations:* A grading rubric for discussion forums clearly delineates good responses from poor responses.
- *Success opportunities:* A practice exam reflects the breadth and depth of content that the actual examination covers.

- *Personal responsibility:* Students are allowed to submit their assignments within a certain time period so that they can decide when they perform best.

Satisfaction

The **satisfaction** aspect of the ARCS model relates to students feeling a sense of accomplishment or achievement. Feedback and reinforcement are two important components of satisfaction. Keller identified three strategies to promote satisfaction: intrinsic satisfaction, rewarding outcomes, and fair treatment. Intrinsic satisfaction refers to students feeling an internal sense of enjoyment from the activities they perform. Rewarding outcomes refers to students receiving concrete feedback and/or recognition for their work. Fair treatment refers to consistency in learning standards and outcomes of success. The following are examples of each category:

- *Intrinsic satisfaction:* An instructor allows students to improve their work after receiving feedback as a means to exhibit their personal best.
- *Rewarding outcomes:* An instructor highlights exemplary work and provides encouraging feedback to students.
- *Fair treatment:* An instructor consistently provides feedback on all work submitted in a timely manner.

Summary

Course authors can effectively use the ARCS Model of Motivational Design to create assignments that motivate students. Many of the principles set forth in the ARCS model are consistent with other instructional design models, such as Robert Gagne's Nine Events of Instruction. ARCS, therefore, is merely one approach to the design of effective instruction. While other models exist, ARCS has a memorable acronym and clear principles, making it one of the easiest approaches to course design that course authors of varying experience can understand and implement.

References

Keller, J. M. (2009). *Motivational design for learning and performance: The ARCS model approach.* New York: Springer.

SECTION IV
COPYRIGHT AND OTHER CONSIDERATIONS

**Chapter 8:
Copyright Basics**

Copyright Law and School Policies

By Mimi O'Malley

Copyright acts as an **intellectual property** protection for creators who transfer ideas or concepts into a fixed, tangible form. In addition to text, tangible forms include disk, canvas, CD-ROM, and film. Designed to grant legal protection for original creators, copyright does not require that copyright holders affix a copyright symbol (©) upon creation. Nor does it require that they register their work with the U.S. Copyright Office or pay a copyright fee. In addition, creators can copyright their work whether or not they publish it. The following chart prepared by Hirtle (2011) at Cornell Copyright Information Center details the copyright terms:

WORKS REGISTERED OR FIRST PUBLISHED IN THE UNITED STATES		
DATE OF PUBLICATION	**CONDITIONS**	**COPYRIGHT TERM**
Before 1923	None	None. In the public domain due to copyright expiration
1923 through 1977	Published without a copyright notice	None. In the public domain due to failure to comply with required formalities
1978 to 1 March 1989	Published without notice and without subsequent registration within 5 years	None. In the public domain due to failure to comply with required formalities
1978 to 1 March 1989	Published without notice but with subsequent registration within 5 years	70 years after the death of author. If a work of corporate authorship, 95 years from publication or 120 years from creation, whichever expires first
1923 through 1963	Published with notice but copyright was not renewed	None. In the public domain due to copyright expiration
1923 through 1963	Published with notice and the copyright was renewed	95 years after publication date
1964 through 1977	Published with notice	95 years after publication date
1978 to 1 March 1989	Created after 1977 and published with notice	70 years after the death of author. If a work of corporate authorship, 95 years from publication or 120 years from creation, whichever expires first

WORKS REGISTERED OR FIRST PUBLISHED IN THE UNITED STATES		
DATE OF PUBLICATION	**CONDITIONS**	**COPYRIGHT TERM**
1978 to 1 March 1989	Created before 1978 and first published with notice during the specified period	The greater of the term specified in the previous entry or 31 December 2047
1 March 1989 through 2002	Created after 1977	70 years after the death of author. If a work of corporate authorship, 95 years from publication or 120 years from creation, whichever expires first
1 March 1989 through 2002	Created before 1978 and first published in this period	The greater of the term specified in the previous entry or 31 December 2047
After 2002	None	70 years after the death of author. If a work of corporate authorship, 95 years from publication or 120 years from creation, whichever expires first
Anytime	Works prepared by an officer or employee of the United States government as part of that person's official duties	None. In the public domain in the United States

Unlike other areas of law, intellectual property law originated almost exclusively within the federal realm, which means that copyright is not subject to state, local, or county regulation (Enghagen, 2005, p. 9). The U.S. Constitution states the following about intellectual property law:

> Congress shall have [the] power…[t]o promote the progress of science and the useful arts, by securing for limited times to authors and inventors the exclusive right to their respective writings and discoveries…As a matter of constitutional law, not only is Congress granted this power, but it is given a specific framework in which to operate (Article I, Section 8, Clause 8).

For corporate authorship (e.g., motion pictures in which numerous individuals participated in the creation of the work), copyright lasts 95 years from the date of creation. For works made for hire, anonymous works, and pseudonymous works (unless the

COPYRIGHT
Legal protection for original creators.

INTELLECTUAL PROPERTY
Ideas or concepts transformed into a fixed, tangible form.

PUBLIC DOMAIN
Pertains to works that have either an expired copyright or no copyright restrictions; also called copyleft.

FAIR USE DOCTRINE
Law that permits limited use of copyrighted works for education, criticism, commentary, news reporting, scholarship, and research without requiring the permission of or payment to the copyright owner.

author's identity appears in U.S. Copyright Office records), the duration of copyright is 95 years from the date of publication or 120 years from the date of creation, whichever is shorter (U.S. Copyright Office, 2008).

Works that are not copyrighted are considered **public domain**. Anyone may use public domain works without the originator's or copyright owner's consent. Original works published before 1923 are also in the public domain in the United States, and you can freely copy these works. In addition, for any work published before 1964, if the copyright holder did not renew the copyright, the work is now in the public domain.

Rights of Copyright Holders
Copyright holders have exclusive rights to do or authorize others to do the following with their copyrighted works:

- Make copies.
- Distribute the work.
- Display the work.
- Perform the work publicly.
- Create other works based on the original work (i.e., derivative works).

These rights allow copyright holders to solicit a fee from others to use or modify their copyrighted work. In addition, copyright holders may bequeath copyright as personal property to their heirs or transfer copyright to another individual or organization (U.S. Copyright Office, 2008). However, these rights are not exclusive; users also have rights to use copyrighted material in certain circumstances.

Copyright Interpretation in Education
In developing copyright law, the Founding Fathers recognized that creators and inventors needed an incentive for undertaking risky (i.e., often unsuccessful) endeavors. With this understanding, they gave creators and inventors a monopoly that represented exclusive rights. They theorized that at least some creators would succeed at some of their endeavors enough to make a living at creating and, therefore, continue generating other creations (Enghagen, 2005, p. 11). Society benefits from such innovation; therefore, social policy in the form of copyright law should encourage it.

At the same time, the innovations that benefit society often have their roots in academic scholarship, which thrives upon communication (in the form of publishing) between peer researchers in a field of study. Without the ability to publish new research, academia is dramatically thwarted in publishing new research or innovation for those creators who thrive on new research. This issue plagues modern-day scholarly communication.

Along with valuing academic research and scholarship, the Founding Fathers believed that the public should have access to creations, many of which stem from education. Section 106 of the Copyright Act defines the right to perform or display a work as the exclusive right of the copyright holder. However, the Copyright Act also provides exceptions under which users do not have to ask permission to use, perform, or display a work. One of these exceptions is the fair use exception contained in Section 107 (Armatas, 2008, p. 214).

The fair use exception permits public access by allowing limited use of copyrighted works for education, criticism, commentary, news reporting, scholarship, and research without requiring the permission of or payment to the copyright owner. Proper use for one of these purposes does not constitute an unlawful copyright infringement (Enghagen, 2005, p. 11). This language provides flexibility for educators to use copyrighted works while balancing the copyright holder's rights to sustain a profit. Courts use the following four criteria, or factors, to determine whether a person or institution may use a work without permission under the **fair use doctrine**:

1. Purpose and character of the use
2. Nature of the copyrighted work
3. Amount and substantiality used in comparison to the work as a whole
4. Effect on potential market for or value of the work

During a fair use court case, the judge decides if each factor favors the plaintiff or the defendant and then makes a ruling (Graesser, Heller, & Strand, 2010). Courts look favorably on **transformative use**, or use that involves a changed or modified form of the original copyrighted work. Thus, transformative use should help instructors feel comfortable using copyrighted material for digital presentations, media, or images. Note also that fair use applies to both nonprofit and for-profit

The American Library Association Office for Information Technology developed a digital copyright slider to help you decipher whether or not the material you want to use in course development may be protected by copyright.

You can find this tool at the following URL:

http://librarycopyright.net/digitalslider/

organizations. The following table from can help in determining how courts view each of the fair use factors (Graesser, Heller, & Strand, 2010):

KEY TERMS

TRANSFORMATIVE USE
Use that involves a changed or modified form of the original copyrighted work.

COPYRIGHT COMPLIANCE
An institution's efforts to obey copyright laws; institutions may have a copyright compliance officer, a copyright policy, or both.

COPYRIGHT POLICY
General statement of compliance with copyright law that recognizes that the law places several limitations on the copyright holder's rights and how these rights and limitations pertain to distance-learning issues.

FAIR USE CRITERIA	DEFINITION	COURTS FAVOR	COURTS FROWN ON
Purpose of the use	Nonprofit vs. commercial; transformative use	Nonprofit and educational use; transformative works	For-profit or commercial use
Character of the use	Criticism, commentary, news reporting, parody, other transformative use	Nonprofit and educational use; transformative works	For-profit or commercial use
Nature of the copyrighted work	Factual in nature (e.g., scholarly, technical, scientific) vs. creative expression	Historical use	Creative expression
Amount and substantiality used in comparison to the work as a whole	The amount and substance of a work one uses; substance of a work includes the "heart of a work" (e.g., the chariot scene in the movie *Ben Hur*)	Smaller portions of a work	Larger amounts of a work; using key scenes or the "heart of the work"
Effect on potential market for or value of the work	The potential to negatively affect the market for or the value of the copyrighted work	Digitizing or copying for educational purposes as long as the copy or digitization is not sold	Digitizing or copying with the potential for sale or profit

The following guidelines clarify the portion limitations of a single copyrighted work and the variance among media:

MEDIA	FAIR USE LIMITS
Text	Up to 10% of the original work or 1,000 words, whichever is less
Poems	Up to 250 words but further limited to the following: • Three poems or portions of poems by one poet • Five poems or portions of poems by different poets from a single anthology
Music	Up to 10% of the original work or 30 seconds, whichever is less
Photos and images	Up to five works per artist or photographer or up to 10% or 15 works of a collection, whichever is less
Database information	Up to 10% or 2,500 fields or cell entries, whichever is less

(Wherry, 2002, p. 168-169)

School Copyright Policies

Even if your institution does not have a **copyright compliance** officer, you should require a copyright policy for the education of staff, faculty members, and students. A **copyright policy** should begin with a general statement that the organization's policy calls for compliance with copyright law and the **copyright holder's** exclusive rights. The policy should also recognize that the law places several limitations on the copyright holder's rights (e.g., the fair use limitation) and indicate that the organization will take full advantage of these limitations. School copyright policies should include discussion of distance-learning issues such as the following (Gasaway, 2006, p. 34-35):

- The extent to which the institution will exercise its fair use privilege
- The extent to which the institution uses interlibrary lending
- The posting of copyrighted materials on the learning management system (LMS)
- The posting of copyrighted works on the Internet

- Where to locate information about institutional licenses for copyrighted works and what you can and cannot do under the license
- How copyrighted materials will be made available to students at nonprofit educational institutions and available for classroom use and distance education

In accordance with the Technology, Education, and Copyright Harmonization (TEACH) Act, your institution should upload its copyright policy onto its LMS and its intranet. You should communicate regularly with your campus librarian for any copyright law or institutional policy updates and incorporate such revisions into your course LMS.

Researchers have noted that many institutional copyright policies lack clarity about fair use guidelines. Sun and Baez (2009) report a more disconcerting fact that existing copyright policies were actually overly restrictive with fair use guidelines (p. 34). Because of heightened concern over litigation, such restrictions may produce pedagogical costs that inadvertently promote less effective teaching methods, according to Sun and Baez (2009, p. 34). Both faculty members and administrators can benefit from creating a copyright policy that balances fair use guidelines and permission for use. This balance minimizes the time necessary to secure a copyrighted work.

Who is in charge of copyright compliance? The answer to this question varies according to each institution. Individuals who know more about copyright and intellectual property tend to be the ones who negotiate software licenses, subscription licensing fees, grants, and permission to use policies. Librarians, instructional technologists, media centers, technology transfer offices, offices of sponsored programs, institutional grant writers, and provosts may serve as sources for copyright compliance.

At Penn State's Department of Distance Education, instructional design staff members specify the rules related to copyright before course development begins (Colyer, 2000, p. 115). For situations in which designers come across copyrighted material embedded in the course, they must return the material to the faculty member so he or she can identify the source from which to obtain permission. Another option is for the faculty member to rewrite the material to address the key points of the original work (Colyer, 2000, p. 115). The Center for Online Learning and Academic

Technology at Friends University helps answer questions about obtaining permission for use, but it maintains that each department must secure its own permissions (M. Sanborn, personal communication, November 15, 2010).

If course materials are produced with grant or external funds of any kind, then the institution's copyright and intellectual property issues related to the particular grant or funding agency must be examined for copyright ownership clarification (Colyer, 2000, p. 115). Questions that the grant officer or office of sponsored programs should investigate include the following (Colyer, 2000, p. 115):

- Does the institution own the copyright on the product?
- Does the outside granting organization or funding source own the copyright?
- Do terms of the grant limit the use, sale, or distribution of any content that has been produced?

Conclusion

As one of the largest stakeholders in copyright compliance, higher education institutions must monitor faculty, student, and staff activities concerning intellectual property. Likewise, as purveyors of research and new knowledge higher education institutions must take an interest in copyright creation as well as intellectual property. Because distance education promotes academic study in the virtual environment, institutions that offer such programs must emphasize even more so the education of both faculty members and online students regarding these issues. Instructors often plagiarize peer faculty members' copyrighted material from other campuses or universities as they build their course content, and online students who plagiarize tend to think that no one is watching as they incorporate copyrighted material into their personal social media pages. Thus, higher education institutions must educate their faculty members, staff, and students about appropriate intellectual property policy.

References

Armatas, S. A. (2008). *Distance learning and copyright: A guide to legal issues*. Chicago: American Bar Association.

Aside from helping schools secure permission to use copyrighted works, the Copyright Clearance Center includes a section on building a copyright compliance plan. You can find this information at

http://www.copyright.com

Colyer, A. (2000). Copyright law, the Internet, and distance education. In M. Moore & G. Cozine (Eds.), *Web-based communications, the Internet, and distance education* (pp. 109-120). University Park, PA: The American Center for the Study of Distance Education.

Enghagen, L. (2005). *Fair use: Guidelines for educators.* Newburyport, MA: Sloan Consortium.

Gasaway, L. N. (2006). *Get copyright right.* Alexandria, VA: Special Libraries Association.

Graesser, C., Heller, J., & Strand, J. (2010, December 7). *Managing copyright in the digital age.* Retrieved May 3, 2011, from http://units.sla.org/division/dleg/2010Programs/copyright-webinar.pdf

Hirtle, P. (2011, January 3). *Copyright term and the public domain in the United States: 1 January 2011.* Retrieved January 12, 2011, from http://copyright.cornell.edu/resources/publicdomain.cfm

Sun, J., & Baez, B. (2009). Intellectual property in the information age: Knowledge as commodity and its legal implications for higher education. *ASHE Higher Education Report, 34*(4), 31-53.

U.S. Copyright Office. (2008, July). *Copyright basics.* Retrieved November 10, 2010, from http://www.copyright.gov/circs/circ1.pdf

Wherry, T. (2002). *The librarian's guide to intellectual property in the digital age: Patents, copyrights and trademarks.* Chicago: American Library Association.

The TEACH Act

By Mimi O'Malley

Persistent problems concerning audiovisual works and the transmission of copyrighted materials in distance learning prompted the passage of the **Technology, Education, and Copyright Harmonization (TEACH) Act** in 2002. This act amended sections 110(2) and 112 of the Copyright Act to facilitate growth and development of digital distance education. Specifically, the TEACH Act increased the number and types of copyrighted works an instructor could use without obtaining permission, paying licensing fees, or relying on items in the public domain (Armatas, 2008, p. 74).

Such exceptions to copyright law were subsequently balanced by numerous restrictions and limitations, including technological restrictions on accessing and copying works; a need to adopt and disseminate copyright policies and information resources; limits on the quantity of certain works that an educator or institution can digitize and include in distance learning; and limits on the use of copyrighted materials in the context of "mediated instructional activities," in some respects akin to the conduct of a traditional course (Enghagen, 2005, p. 83). Moreover, the TEACH Act extended to users the opportunity to retain archival copies of course materials on servers and the authority to convert some copyrighted works from analog to digital formats. The following illustration explains the three kinds of TEACH Act requirements that impact distance education (Gasaway, 2006, p. 57):

INSTITUTION REQUIREMENTS	INFORMATION TECHNOLOGY REQUIREMENTS	COURSE INSTRUCTOR REQUIREMENTS
• Only U.S. Department of Education-accredited, nonprofit educational institutions and governmental bodies qualify. • Institutions must establish policies for copyright and must communicate to faculty members, staff, and students the importance of complying with copyright law.	• Educators must apply technological measures to safeguard copyrighted works beyond the class session. • Educators must transmit class materials only to students officially enrolled in a course. • Educators must be able to put ephemeral recordings on their servers, which will be displayed for distance education courses. • The Act permits digitizing of certain works.	• The Act allows for unlimited performance of nondramatic literary or musical works and for "reasonable and limited" portions of other types of works. • Performance or display must be made by, at the direction of, or under the actual supervision of an instructor as an integral part of a systemic mediated instructional activity.

TEACH Act: Allowance

The TEACH Act allows audiovisual works in reasonable and limited portions to be available online, but it excludes textbooks, readings, and workbooks from such access. Furthermore, if you obtain permission from the copyright holder to use portions of textbooks, readings, and workbooks, you may use only the specific materials for which you received permission to use (Simpson, 2005, p. 165). The following table discusses the allowable material under the TEACH Act (Enghagen, 2005, p. 83-84; Simpson, 2005, p. 55):

PERMITTED UNDER THE TEACH ACT	EXAMPLES
The TEACH Act allows for the performance of nondramatic literary and musical works in their entirety.	Nondramatic literary works include poetry and short stories. Nondramatic musical works include most musical works other than operas, music videos, and musicals.
The Act permits the transmission of any other performance (including dramatic and audiovisual works).	The portions used must be "limited and reasonable."
The Act permits the transmission of the display of any work as long as the display is comparable to that typically used in face-to-face instruction.	Still images may be transmitted as part of a distance learning course.

VIOLATIONS OF THE TEACH ACT	EXAMPLES
The TEACH Act prohibits instructors from using copyright-protected materials if they know or have reason to believe that the materials were not lawfully made or acquired.	The TEACH Act does not limit this rule to situations in which faculty members unlawfully made or acquired the work. The rule also applies, for example, to a pirated work that someone else made and gave or sold to faculty members.
The Act prohibits faculty members from using the rights granted under the TEACH Act to use copyright-protected works created and marketed for distance learning courses without paying for the right to do so.	This restriction applies to ancillary materials, such as textbooks, course packs, and software that students typically buy for their courses.

The following checklist will guide you toward meeting the TEACH Act requirements so you do not upload copyrighted material onto your online course without first seeking permission to use it (Carnevale, 2003):

- The college must be accredited and nonprofit.
- The college must have an internal policy concerning copyright law and the use of copyrighted material.
- The college must provide to faculty members printed or online resources that describe their rights and responsibilities under copyright law.
- The material must not have been originally intended for educational use.
- The material must have been lawfully acquired.
- The material must be an integral part of the class session.
- Reasonable precautions must be taken to restrict access to the copyrighted content to students who are enrolled in the course.
- Other reasonable controls must be used to prevent students from disseminating the material after viewing it.
- If a digital version of the material is readily available for use at the college, then the instructor cannot convert an analog version to digital form for use in an online course.
- The college must inform students that the material may be protected by copyright law.

TEACH Act: Institutional Obligations

As Armatas (2008) states, the TEACH Act places responsibility for copyright compliance squarely on the shoulders of the educational institution (p. 447). These **institutional obligations** require institutions to impose restrictions on access, develop new policies, and disseminate copyright information. While the TEACH Act does not specifically dictate how the institution must ensure copyright compliance, it does mandate that institutions undertake the three principal measures:

- Implement copyright policies.
- Educate the institution's community about copyright.
- Implement appropriate technological measures to prevent the unauthorized use, access, or distribution of copyright-protected works.

Most experts agree that the likely expectation is that institutions will create and implement policies to guide faculty members and staff as they incorporate copyright-protected works into distance learning classes (Enghagen, 2005, p. 81). As with previous copyright initiatives, flexibility is paramount. Institutions can freely develop and distribute copyright policies in any manner they

TECHNOLOGY, EDUCATION, AND COPYRIGHT HARMONIZATION (TEACH) ACT
A law that increased the number and types of copyrighted works an instructor can use without obtaining permission, paying licensing fees, or relying on items in the public domain.

INSTITUTIONAL OBLIGATIONS
TEACH Act requirements that institutions be responsible for copyright compliance by imposing their own restrictions on access, developing new policies, and disseminating copyright information.

deem appropriate, including via written materials, face-to-face workshops, distance learning instruction, or websites.

From a technological perspective, the TEACH Act focuses on the course content's security. The Act requires that institutions and their educators transmit course content for the sole use of enrolled students. In most cases, courses delivered via learning management systems (LMSs) are password-protected and restricted to registered students, thereby avoiding the issue of unauthorized access. However, other course content made available to students online may not meet this requirement for limited access (Enghagen, 2005, p. 82). For example, you may consider developing a personal blog for your students through Blogger.com, even though websites that are not secure do not satisfy the security requirement, because anyone may access and transmit the content rather than just registered students. Therefore, you should avoid posting copyright-protected works to sites that are not secure.

One of the greatest misconceptions about copyrighted works and the Internet relates to copying. Transmission of material via the Internet may or may not involve the automatic creation of copies. For example, a live open- or closed-circuit television broadcast does not involve copying, but computer network communications do. When material is sent electronically, temporary RAM copies are made in the computers through which the transmission passes. The version the recipient receives is a copy of the original material. This is the essence of how a digital network operates. The courts have consistently held that RAM copies impede the copyright owner's reproduction rights (Armatas, 2008, p. 406).

Specifically related to online course development, the TEACH Act addresses time, storage, and dissemination of copyrighted material. In particular, the TEACH Act focuses on limiting the retention of copyright-protected works beyond the time required for the course. The Act also addresses outside interference with measures that copyright owners can take to control the storage and dissemination of their works (e.g., authentication logins). Generally, the institution's information technology department is responsible for developing and implementing practices and procedures for compliance with the technologically oriented requirements of the TEACH Act (Enghagen, 2005, p. 83). The following table presents a few considerations related to uploading copyrighted works into an LMS course shell (Blackboard, 2000, p. 5):

PORTION	DISTRIBUTION	TIME
Make sure the portions of copyrighted works meet fair use guidelines.	Store copyrighted materials in a secure location within your LMS.	Make copyrighted material available for no more than 15 days on the LMS course shell.
Use the fair use *four factor* criteria.	Avoid putting copyrighted material on your personal Web pages.	Use the *Availability from dates* function in your LMS.

If you are deciding whether or not to use copyrighted material, refer to the fair use *four factor* criteria: purpose and character of use, nature of copyrighted work, amount and substantiality used in comparison to the work as a whole, and the effect on potential market for or value of the work. Courts will look favorably on works that have been changed or modified from the original copyrighted work, which is defined as transformative use. Thus, transformative use should help you feel comfortable using copyrighted material to create digital presentations, media, or images.

You can approach the implementation of the TEACH Act in two ways. First, you can cite fair use and circumvent implementation of the TEACH Act and incorporate only public domain resources into online courses. Pursuing this path may mean limiting instructors to mostly historical rather than current resources. For subjects such as science, medicine, and technology, this approach is imprudent and does not align with the pursuit of federal research grant funding. Conversely, you may promulgate the TEACH Act, require permission to use material from copyright owners, and limit the number of distance learning course offerings (Armatas, 2008, p. 448). Securing permission to use a copyrighted work may take up to several months, depending on the situation. This timetable may overlap with the launch of a course. The following table provides guidelines that describe the portion limitations (which vary depending on the type of media) on a single copyrighted work:

MEDIA	FAIR USE LIMITS
Text	Up to 10% of the original work or 1,000 words, whichever is less
Poems	Up to 250 words but further limited to the following: Three poems or portions of poems by one poet or five poems or portions of poems by different poets from a single anthology
Music	Up to 10% of the original work or 30 seconds, whichever is less
Photos and images	Up to five works per artist or photographer or up to 10% or 15 works of a collection, whichever is less
Database information	Up to 10% or 2,500 fields or cell entries, whichever is less

(Wherry, 2002, p. 168-169)

References

Armatas, S. A. (2008). *Distance learning and copyright: A guide to legal issues*. Chicago: American Bar Association.

Blackboard. (2000). *Copyright, fair use, and educational multimedia FAQ*. Retrieved November 14, 2010, from http://www.ccsj.edu/blackboard/BB%20copyright_fair_use.pdf

Carnevale, D. (2003, March 28). Slow start for long-awaited easing of copyright restriction. *The Chronicle of Higher Education*, *49*(29), A29-A31.

Enghagen, L. (2005). *Fair use: Guidelines for educators*. Newburyport, MA: Sloan Consortium.

Gasaway, L. N. (2006). *Get copyright right*. Alexandria, VA: Special Libraries Association.

Simpson, C. (2005). *Copyright catechism: Practical answers to everyday dilemmas*. Worthington, OH: Linworth Publishing.

Wherry, T. (2002). *The librarian's guide to intellectual property in the digital age: Patents, copyrights and trademarks*. Chicago: American Library Association.

Chapter 9:
Avoiding Copyright Infringement

Open Content and Public Domain Works

By Mimi O'Malley

Education, like technology, has undergone a transformation in recent years due in large part to the way information sharing has changed. The Internet has provided a vehicle for experts around the world to collaborate asynchronously on projects at little to no cost. Today, the idea of open, uninhibited collaboration permeates all sectors of education, and scholars at even the most renowned universities seek to share their knowledge with the masses through open content.

The term **open content** refers to content that is free for public distribution without exclusive rights. Like open-source software, open content exists as a community resource for the masses to use, reuse, and improve. Open content, however, is not a license. It is a concept. Open content can be licensed in a number of ways, although the two most common open content license types are public domain and creative commons.

What Are Public Domain Works?

Public domain works are those that have either an expired copyright or no copyright restrictions. Most created works have a copyright holder or multiple copyright holders who have the exclusive right to do or authorize others to do certain things with their copyrighted works, including the following:

- Make copies.
- Distribute the work.
- Display the work.
- Perform the work publicly.
- Create other works based on the original work (i.e., derivative works).

These rights, however, create only a limited monopoly and are not absolute (Enghagen, 2005, p. 16). Copyright law does permit free access to the use of copyright-protected works under certain circumstances. First, you may use works without obtaining permission from or paying a fee to the copyright holder if the copyright has expired. Second, you may use copyrighted works without obtaining permission if the use fits the criteria for fair use. Third, you may use copyrighted works without permission or payment when the works are in the public domain.

The copyright (left) and the public domain (right) symbols

When a copyright expires, the work moves into the public domain, also known as copyleft. At that point, copyright law no longer protects the original work. Consequently, the public can use it without permission from or payment to the owner (Enghagen, 2005, p. 12). While copyright holders have certain exclusive privileges to reproduce, distribute, perform, and display their creations, no one has these exclusive privileges for works in the public domain. Thus, public domain works have no restrictions on who can reproduce, distribute, perform, or display them. With no ownership rights associated with public domain works, everyone and no one owns the work (Gasaway, 2006, p. 5).

A work may fall into the public domain category for several reasons, including the following (Fishman, 2010, p. 5):
- The work was published prior to enactment of the copyright law.
- The work's copyright protection expired.
- Copyright protection was lost or never acquired for whatever reason.
- The copyright owner dedicated the work to the public domain.
- The work was never entitled to copyright protection.

How to Know If a Work Is in the Public Domain

To fully understand whether or not a work falls into the public domain, knowledge of basic information about copyright law is essential. All U.S. works published before 1923 are in the public domain in the United States. In addition to pre-1923 works, millions of other works have fallen into the public domain because the copyright holder either failed to renew the copyright or failed to affix a proper notice on the work (Jessin, 2010). In the United States, the length of copyright protection that a work receives depends on when the work was created. The following table details the copyright terms for works registered or first published in the United States (Hirtle, 2011):

WORKS REGISTERED OR FIRST PUBLISHED IN THE UNITED STATES		
DATE OF PUBLICATION	**CONDITIONS**	**COPYRIGHT TERM**
Before 1923	None	None. In the public domain due to copyright expiration
1923 through 1977	Published without a copyright notice	None. In the public domain due to failure to comply with required formalities
1978 to 1 March 1989	Published without notice and without subsequent registration within 5 years	None. In the public domain due to failure to comply with required formalities
1978 to 1 March 1989	Published without notice but with subsequent registration within 5 years	70 years after the death of author. If a work of corporate authorship, 95 years from publication or 120 years from creation, whichever expires first

WORKS REGISTERED OR FIRST PUBLISHED IN THE UNITED STATES		
DATE OF PUBLICATION	CONDITIONS	COPYRIGHT TERM
1923 through 1963	Published with notice but copyright was not renewed	None. In the public domain due to copyright expiration
1923 through 1963	Published with notice and the copyright was renewed	95 years after publication date
1964 through 1977	Published with notice	95 years after publication date
1978 to 1 March 1989	Created after 1977 and published with notice	70 years after the death of author. If a work of corporate authorship, 95 years from publication or 120 years from creation, whichever expires first
1978 to 1 March 1989	Created before 1978 and first published with notice during the specified period	The greater of the term specified in the previous entry or 31 December 2047
1 March 1989 through 2002	Created after 1977	70 years after the death of author. If a work of corporate authorship, 95 years from publication or 120 years from creation, whichever expires first
1 March 1989 through 2002	Created before 1978 and first published in this period	The greater of the term specified in the previous entry or 31 December 2047
After 2002	None	70 years after the death of author. If a work of corporate authorship, 95 years from publication or 120 years from creation, whichever expires first
Anytime	Works prepared by an officer or employee of the United States government as part of that person's official duties	None. In the public domain in the United States

You should assume that a work is copyrighted unless you have evidence that it is not. Public domain works usually display the public domain symbol or contain a written public domain notice.

However, if a work does not display the public domain symbol or contain a public domain disclaimer and you believe that it is in the public domain, you have some options available to help you determine the copyright status of the work. For works published between 1923 and 1963, you can investigate whether the copyright was renewed by contacting the U.S. Copyright Office. For a fee of approximately $150 per hour, the **U.S. Copyright Office** will search its public records and provide a report of its findings. Such searches, however, have their limits and do not always produce conclusive results (Ebbinghouse, 2008). In addition, the U.S. Copyright Office takes 6 to 8 weeks to conduct the search and furnish a report. You also can request an expedited search, which takes 5 business days and costs $445. In either case, your search could be worthwhile in light of a 1961 U.S. Copyright Office study that found that less than 15% of all registered copyrights had been renewed; for books, less than 7% had been renewed (Hirtle, 2011).

A qualified copyright search firm or intellectual property attorney can also run a renewal status search. For works published between 1950 and 1963, you can conduct a renewal search online. Researching works that originated between 1923 and 1949, however, requires more time and effort because you must manually search the U.S. Copyright Office Catalog of Copyright Entries in a library that has a copy of this catalog or at the U.S. Copyright Office (Fishman, 2010, p. 392). No matter who completes the search, the researcher should seek the following information (Jessin, 2010):

- Date the work was published or registered
- Name of the person or entity who created the work
- Title of the work (and any possible name variants)
- Where the work was first published
- Copyright certificate number

COPYRIGHT RENEWAL RATES (1958–59)	
TYPE OF WORK	**RENEWAL PERCENTAGE**
Books	7
Periodicals	11
Lectures, speeches, sermons, and other works for oral delivery	0.4
Drama	11
Music	35
Maps	48
Works of art	4
Technical drawings	0.4
Art prints	4
Movies	74

Chapter 21: Researching Copyright Office Records, 2010

Always begin your search by examining the document for a copyright notice and date (e.g., © 1929 by John Smith). The date of the copyright notice usually indicates the work's publication date (Jessin, 2010). Some copyright notices also include the copyright renewal date (e.g., © 1929 by Damon Runyon. Renewed 1956 by Damon Runyon, Jr. and Mary Runyon McCann); in such cases, you do not need to conduct a renewal search.

Unfortunately, a database that identifies works in the public domain does not exist. However, the website The Online Books Page (http://onlinebooks.library.upenn.edu/okbooks.html) maintains a list of more than 900,000 public domain books on the Internet; a list for renewed and nonrenewed U.S. copyrights and other copyrights; and tools for determining whether a work is copyrighted (Ebbinghouse, 2008). The Online Books Page and the following additional resources should help you locate, verify, and digitize a work in the public domain (Ebbinghouse, 2008):

SOURCE	WEBSITE
LLRX.com's Library Digitization Projects and Copyright: Part I: Introduction and Overview	http://www.llrx.com/features/digitization.htm#TOC
Stanford University Libraries' Public Domain Trouble Spots	http://fairuse.stanford.edu/Copyright_and_Fair_Use_Overview/chapter8/8-b.html
Project Gutenberg	http://www.gutenberg.org

(Ebbinghouse, 2008)

Where to Find Public Domain Resources

One of the first places to look for public domain resources is the federal government. Works created by U.S. government employees or officers fall into the public domain category. However, the federal government may contract with third-party vendors to produce materials; in those instances, the third party retains the copyright (Enghagen, 2005, p. 17). Thus, you should always look for a copyright notice that indicates private ownership even when searching federal government materials. In addition, as Fishman (2010) acknowledged in his book on copyright, public domain federal government works do not necessarily translate into works that the public can access (p. 47). Many government documents are classified for national security reasons and are unavailable to the public. For example, the public does not have access to personal or sensitive documents from the CIA, the FBI, the State Department, the IRS, or even the National Institutes of Health. The following table shows the various governmental bodies, and thus, substantial information that may come from these governmental entities.

FEDERAL GOVERNMENT	50 STATE GOVERNMENTS	87,000+ LOCAL GOVERNMENTS
Executive branch, Congress, U.S. Supreme Court, federal courts, IRS, Department of Defense, U.S. Copyright Office	State governors, state capitols, state legislatures, state courts, state agencies (such as the Department of Motor Vehicles)	City, county, village, borough, mayors, city councils, city agencies (such as the local school district)

While works that federal government employees create fall into the public domain category, state and local government employees may claim copyright to the works they produce. If in doubt of usage rights, call the agency that provided the work and verify that the material was produced by a state, local, or federal government agency.

Several websites index public domain resources as well, but you will need to do some sleuthing to verify that works are truly in the public domain. The safest course of action is to assume that the material is copyrighted unless you find evidence that it is in the public domain. Wikimedia.com indexes some public domain images, maps, charts, graphs, and similar material. Likewise, Google™ Advanced Search feature (see illustration) allows you to limit a search to websites, images, videos, and the like with free-to-use usage rights. You also may want to add the U.S. National Library of Medicine, Internet Archive, and Public Library of Science websites to your browser favorites when you seek public domain resources.

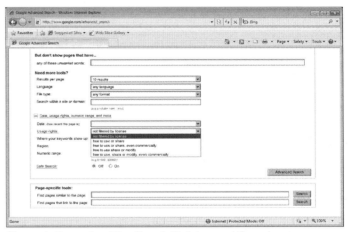

Figure 1. Example of the Google™ Advanced Search page.

When you search any website, you must scan the entire Web page for evidence of copyright before using the material. If you have any doubt about the copyright, seek permission to use the material.

What Are Creative Commons Works?

In addition to public domain works, **Creative Commons** works also fall into the open content category. Two Duke University professors, Larry Lessig and James Boyle, launched Creative Commons in 2001 to encourage creators to make their original

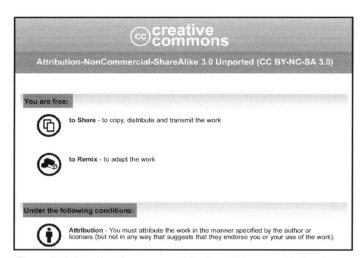

Figure 2. A Creative Commons attribution Web page. Notice that you can freely use the material under certain conditions.

work accessible and affordable to users online (Gasaway, 2006, p. 10). Creative Commons (see Figure 2) offers several license types to copyright holders, ranging from those that allow users to completely edit works for commercial and noncommercial use to those that allow users only to distribute the works as they stand. All Creative Commons licenses, however, allow for free distribution of content bearing that license type.

What Cannot Be Copyrighted?

Not all material is copyrighted. For example, facts do not constitute an original creation, so they are in the public domain. The arrangement of facts (e.g., document, graphs, presentations), however, is original and thus copyrighted. Laws are also in the public domain category, as are short phrases (e.g., *Bon voyage* or *How's it going?*). However, if a company uses a short phrase in advertising a product or service (e.g., *Got milk?*), the phrase might fit the criteria for a trademark and be covered under trademark law (Ebbinghouse, 2008).

You cannot copyright ideas—such as scientific theories, mathematic formulas, and plotlines (e.g., boy meets girl, boy loses girl, boy gets girl)—but you can copyright the expression of the ideas. For example, you can copyright a scientific article in a magazine, a movie script, or the text of a novel or short story with a plot similar to that of another story because the story's expression and characters are original (Ebbinghouse, 2008). The following table lists additional materials in the public domain category:

TYPE OF MATERIAL	PUBLIC DOMAIN	COPYRIGHT
Federal, state, local or foreign laws	☑	Not applicable
Databases (e.g., student class roster)	Facts	Arrangement and selection of facts
Blank forms	☑	Not applicable
Standard calendars	☑	Photos, images, and illustrations within a calendar

TYPE OF MATERIAL	PUBLIC DOMAIN	COPYRIGHT
Height and weight charts	☑	Not applicable
Tape measures and rulers	☑	Not applicable
Frequently asked questions (FAQ) pages	☑	Not applicable
Typefaces	☑	Computer software used to generate typefaces
Food and drink recipes	☑	Not applicable

(Fishman, 2010, p. 316)

What Other Open Content Works May Have Copyright Protection?

Dramatic works (e.g., movies) have multiple copyright holders. Therefore, even though one copyright holder may not have renewed his or her copyright for the movie, another copyright holder may have secured additional rights of usage. Also, other countries have longer periods of copyright protection than the United States does, so works in the public domain in the United States might still have copyright protection abroad and vice versa (Ebbinghouse, 2008). Some works first published outside of the United States have been rescued from the public domain by a variety of treaties; however, these works must meet certain qualifications. As Ebbinghouse (2008) recommends, you should always research a work's public domain status in each country where you plan to publish or display the work. Alternatively, you can follow the lead of someone who has already cleared the path by checking the availability status of material at Project Gutenberg (http://www.gutenberg.org/wiki/Main_Page) or Google Books (http://books.google.com).

In addition, while compilations may include public domain works that remain in the public domain even when compiled, the selection, coordination, and arrangement of the material may be unique enough for the work as a whole to receive its own copyright protection as a compilation (Ebbinghouse, 2008). Anyone can copy a few or all of the public domain portions, arrange them another way, and include other public domain materials. Likewise, anyone can add his or her own copyrightable contribution (e.g., a narrative or commentary) to public domain materials.

Advantages and Challenges of Open Content

If copyright law was designed to pique creators' and inventors' potential for innovation, public domain was established to balance the potential for creators to hold a monopoly on their works (Enghagen, 2005, p. 11). In truth, those who place their creative works in the public domain actually extend the potential for the public to view their work rather than limit the audience to journal, magazine, or newspaper subscription holders.

One way that faculty members promote student scholarship is by encouraging the use of open content materials. If these open content materials were copyrighted, students would have to seek permission before using any part of an original work and, in some circumstances, pay a fee for use. Because students follow an academic calendar, trying to obtain permission to use copyrighted materials would be problematic in terms of time. In addition, most cash-strapped students would opt not to pay for copyrighted works. Thus, public domain resources often serve as the best choice for student use. The following table shows the balancing act between public domain works and copyrighted works:

PUBLIC DOMAIN	COPYRIGHT
Inspires new works	Promotes innovation
Fosters scholarship and artistic freedom	Gives creators incentive to create
	Creates a monopoly of intellectual property

Further strengthening the argument for promoting open content resources is the notion that open content and learning preferences have a mutual relationship. Research has proven that different students learn differently: visually, aurally, kinesthetically, or a mixture of all three learning styles (Gardner, Jewler, & Barefoot, 2009, p. 42). Using open content learning objects that satisfy each of these learning preferences offers instructors more flexibility in their teaching. For example, *Biology Workbench* is an open-source project collection of teaching and learning resources centering on the analysis of molecular sequence and structure data (Bruce, 2003). This project allows users to access an online repository of works ranging from visuals (such as a mutated region of a molecule alignment between proteins and genes) to scholarly articles in a digital library. In the rapidly changing field of science, *Biology Workbench* has provided pharmaceutical companies and universities with an intellectual knowledge base that likely would have taken years to develop had the content been published in traditional scholarly communication venues (Bruce, 2003).

Aside from the cost benefit, using open content resources frees you from spending time seeking permission to use original works. If you have little time or few resources to develop an original creation, the use of open content resources may best fit your situation, especially because the process of securing permission to use material usually takes several weeks. In addition, open content resources free you from needing to seek future permission from a copyright holder who grants permission for only a specific period. If a copyright holder does grant you permission to use an original work, you must be sure to verify whether the permission to use that work expires. If it does expire, then you must reapply for permission or find another source when the permission expires.

Time and cost rate as the strongest factors for using open content resources, but such resources may not always be the best fit for your needs. For example, most resources available in the public domain date prior to 1923. Such resources provide a wealth of historical topics, but they may not provide the best information for science and technology topics. Conversely, most Creative Commons works are newer and come in digitized form with allowance for modifications or inclusion in another work.

To use open content wisely, always consider the purpose of the work and your students' needs. Carefully select works that address the objectives of your course, and try to incorporate works with commentary rather than using the sources outright. The more you can do to customize open content to address course objectives, the more the open content will benefit students.

References

Bruce, B. (2003). The role, value, and limits of S & T data and information in the public domain for education. In J. M. Esanu & P. F. Uhlir (Eds.), The Role of Scientific and Technical Data and Information in the Public Domain: Proceedings of a Symposium (pp. 56-59). Washington, DC: National Research Council of the National Academies.

Chapter 21: Researching copyright office records. (2010). In S. Fishman (Ed.), *The public domain: How to find & use copyright-free writings, music, art & more* (pp. 387-407). Retrieved May 3, 2011, from the EBSCOhost database.

Ebbinghouse, C. (2008). "Copyfraud" and public domain works. *Searcher, 16*(1), 40. Retrieved January 12, 2011, from EBSCOhost.

Enghagen, L. (2005). *Fair use: Guidelines for educators*. Newburyport, MA: Sloan Consortium.

Fishman, S. (2010). *The public domain: How to find and use copyright-free writings, music, art and more*. Berkeley, CA: Nolo Publishing.

Gardner, J., Jewler, A., & Barefoot, B. (2009). *Your college experience: Strategies for success*. Boston: Wadsworth Cengage Learning.

Gasaway, L. N. (2006). *Get copyright right*. Alexandria, VA: Special Libraries Association.

Hirtle, P. (2011, January 3). *Copyright term and the public domain: 1 January 2011*. Cornell Copyright Information Center. Retrieved December 3, 2010, from http://copyright.cornell.edu/resources/docs/copyrightterm.pdf

Jessin, L. J. (2010). *New rules for using public domain materials*. Retrieved November 18, 2010, from http://www.copylaw.com/new_articles/PublicDomain.html

Requesting Copyright Permission

By Mimi O'Malley

If you need to seek permission to use material in your course, planning and organizing will greatly limit your frustration. Stim (2010) advises that you take the following actions when securing permission to use a work (p. 410):

1. Plan for obtaining permission.
2. Identify the owner.
3. Identify the rights you will need.
4. Negotiate payment.
5. Secure a written agreement.

Planning

Since copyright allows exclusive rights for copyright holders to do or authorize others to use their copyrighted works, you should allow at least 1 to 3 months for obtaining permission to use a copyrighted source. If the copyright holder does grant you permission, be prepared to pay a fee to use the material. Because copyright holders control the rights to reproduce, distribute, and modify their works, they often offer a sliding scale of fees for different rights and uses. If a month passes and you have not heard from the copyright holder about your permission request, consider using another source. You can also contact your department chairperson, dean, or collection development librarian to see if your institution maintains a contract with a license rights organization. A license rights organization will complete much of the permission legwork and handle the paperwork for you or your institution.

LICENSE RIGHTS SPECIALISTS	WEB PAGE
Copyright Clearance Center	http://www.copyright.com/search.do?operation=show&page=ppu
iCopyright	http://info.icopyright.com/

Ownership

Begin by identifying who owns the copyright to the work you want to use. In some circumstances, you may see a copyright symbol displayed on the work (e.g., Copyright © 2010 Globe Pequot Publishing). If you are unable to determine who owns the copyright, you can check with the U.S. Copyright Office or the Copyright Clearance Center. Pieces of art, films, and recorded music often have multiple owners or copyright holders, each with separate rights to different parts of the work (Stim, 2010, p. 412). In such cases, you will need to secure permission from all entities involved in the creation of the copyrighted work.

FINDING A COPYRIGHT HOLDER	WEB PAGE
The University of Texas at Austin's Harry Ransom Center	http://tyler.hrc.utexas.edu/us.cfm#Q6
The Online Books Page	http://digital.library.upenn.edu/books/okbooks.html

Terms

After you have contacted the copyright holder, he or she will want to know the details for your use of the copyrighted work. Determining your intended use before you request permission may save you time, as it will help you avoid having to renegotiate your permission to use the work. Stim (2010) advises that you should include the following three variables when negotiating permission to use a copyrighted work: exclusivity, term, and territory. Conditions for terms of use may be as narrow or as broad as both parties deem necessary.

The copyright holder may choose terms either as an **exclusive agreement** (an agreement in which only one person has the right to use a copyrighted work) or **nonexclusive agreement** (an agreement in which more than one person has the right to use a copyrighted work).

When seeking permission, you should ask for nonexclusive world rights in the English language, including U.S. rights. Make sure you request that the permission cover any electronic versions of the work, any future revisions or editions, and any foreign language translations.

The following table gives more details about each variable:

KEY TERMS

EXCLUSIVE AGREEMENT
Agreement in which only one person has the right to use a copyrighted work.

NONEXCLUSIVE AGREEMENT
Agreement in which more than one person has the right to use a copyrighted work.

COURSE PACKS
Books or articles that publishers allow schools to copy and distribute in educational contexts for a fee and for a limited amount of time (e.g., one semester).

EXCLUSIVE OR NONEXCLUSIVE AGREEMENT	TERMS OF USE	TERRITORY
• Exclusive agreements refer to only one person who has right to use work. • Nonexclusive allows others to use material (language usage, world rights, future editions, and electronic rights).	• Rights of use may be limited by time. No limitation means you have the right to use for as long as copyright isn't revoked. • Terms of use gives permission to use as long as copyright remains.	• Territory limits use to a geographic region. • Contract may need to be renegotiated if you use the work outside of designated territory.

Fees

Some authors charge fees for the use of their work, and those fees are often connected to the popularity of the work. Fees for websites are determined by the number of visitors to the site (Fishman, 2010, p. 410). Depending on the fee structure, you may decide to circumvent paying a fee and choose public domain materials instead. You can always negotiate the fees related to usage; however, the copyright holder makes the final decision.

Written Agreement

Whatever terms you and the copyright holder agree to, make sure you ask for a written copy of the agreement. Misunderstanding and miscommunication of oral agreements can occur. If you have to go to court to enforce your unwritten agreement, you will have difficulty proving the exact terms (Stim, 2010). Also, be sure to store all written agreements in a secure place, such as on a CD-ROM or flash drive.

Course Pack Permission to Use

Whether sold at the campus bookstore or by instructors in class, **course packs** often receive special "clearances" from publishers. That is, for a fee, publishers grant permission for schools to copy and distribute their books or articles in educational contexts (Stanford University Libraries, 2010). Such clearances normally last for one semester or one school term. In addition to paper course packs, some publishers now offer electronic course packs, or portals (e.g., Pearson's MyCompLab™) for use in distance learning. When seeking permission to use these kinds of sources, you should contact the publisher cited on the copyright page of the publication. Do not contact the author, because, in many cases, the publisher, rather than the author, holds the primary rights. If the publisher does not hold the copyright, the publisher's office can tell you who does. Ultimately, the responsibility lies with you to continue searching for all the copyright holders and request permission to use the works in a course pack.

Most instructors do not have the time to seek and obtain permission for the 20 to 30 (or more) articles used in a course pack. Fortunately, private clearance services will, for a fee, acquire permission and assemble course packs on your behalf. After the course packs are created and sold, the clearance service collects royalties and distributes the payments to the holders of the rights (Stanford University Libraries, 2010). Educational institutions may require instructors to use a specific clearance service, so check with your dean or department chairperson first. Some clearance companies also provide clearance for electronic course packs. If you need to use a clearance service, consider contacting one of the following organizations:

COPYRIGHT CLEARANCE COMPANIES	WEB PAGE
Copyright Clearance Center	http://www.copyright.com
XanEdu Publishing	http://www.xanedu.com
University Readers	http://www.universityreaders.com

Assembling Your Own Course Pack

Two good reasons exist for creating your own course pack: (a) A clearance company may not be able to obtain permission for certain items that you may be able to obtain yourself, and (b) By requesting permission yourself, you can save students money by minimizing your fees (Stanford University Libraries, 2010). Clearance companies often affiliate with academic publishers and already have gathered the necessary permissions from these publishers. It is much more efficient to have a license for the entire academic publishing catalog than to secure individual permissions here and there. However, if you choose to use material in your course pack that does not come from an academic press, the clearance company may not try to secure permission or may not be able to obtain permission if it does try (Stanford University Libraries, 2010). The following table lists some issues to consider if you elect to create your own course pack (Stanford University Libraries, 2010):

Go to the publisher (not the author) for the material you want to use.	• Send your request to the publisher's permissions, licensing, or clearance department. • If the publisher does not control the rights you need, the publisher's office probably can direct you to the rights' holder.
Obtain permission for a work even if the work is not in print.	Even if a work is out of print, you still need permission to use the work unless it is in the public domain.

Fax or mail your request at least 3 to 9 weeks before your class begins.	Most publishers will not accept email requests for permission.

For most institutions, the responsibility for obtaining clearance for materials used in class lies with the instructor. Check with your dean or department chairperson to confirm this is the case for your institution. University policies may require that the instructor delegate the task to the campus bookstore, copy shop, or a division of the university that specializes in clearances (Stanford University Libraries, 2010). Instructors typically turn to one of the following for help with permissions: clearance services, university bookstores, university copy shop, and department administration. The following chart offers sample permission to use forms for various instructional materials:

MATERIAL	SAMPLE PERMISSION TO USE	WEB PAGE
Course materials	College of DuPage Library	http://www.cod.edu/library/services/copyright/permissions.htm#Sample
Multimedia or course materials	The University of Texas System Office of General Counsel	http://www.utsystem.edu/OGC/Intellectualproperty/permmm.htm
Student work	Highline Community College	https://flightline.highline.edu/copyright/faculty/student_work.htm
Various	University of Connecticut Libraries	http://www.lib.uconn.edu/copyright/permissions_sampleLetters.html

Options for When You Do Not Seek Permission to Use

Developing an online course may take up to 6 to 8 weeks, and content writers should factor in the process of securing permissions as part of that timetable. Most institutions operate under the rule that if content writers cannot find the publisher and obtain permission, then they should not use the item. When in doubt, seek legal advice; the boundaries of fair use lie at the edges of whatever an organization's lawyers are prepared to defend (Colyer, 1997).

For sources that prove difficult to secure permission for use, you can provide a link to the source online rather than use the actual work. Likewise, you may list key materials (e.g., textbook, course pack) within your syllabus as required and then list the items you have not received permission to use as recommended or optional reading. Face-to-face students can more easily visit the campus library and view course materials on library reserve; however, library reserve is not always an option for distance learners.

Rather than asking for permission to reprint items uploaded onto the institution's learning management system, you may consider having students subscribe to a journal for the duration of the academic term. Some periodicals offer student subscriptions at a heavily discounted rate (Colyer, 1997). Likewise, for film and video clips with multiple copyright holders, you may want to verify that students can rent a copy of the video at a video store rather than upload a clip in your LMS course shell. This approach may take less time than obtaining permission for the uploading of the hyperlink (hence, performance of a work) (Colyer, 1997).

References

Colyer, A. (1997). Copyright law, the Internet, and distance education. *American Journal of Distance Education, 11*(3), 41-57.

Fishman, S. (2010). *The public domain: How to find and use copyright free writings, music, art and more.* Berkeley, CA: Nolo Publishing.

Stanford University Libraries. (2010). *Academic coursepacks.* Retrieved November 18, 2010, from http://fairuse.stanford.edu/Copyright_and_Fair_Use_Overview/chapter7/7-a.html

Stim, R. (2010). *Getting permission: How to license and clear copyrighted materials online and off.* Berkeley, CA: Nolo Publishing.

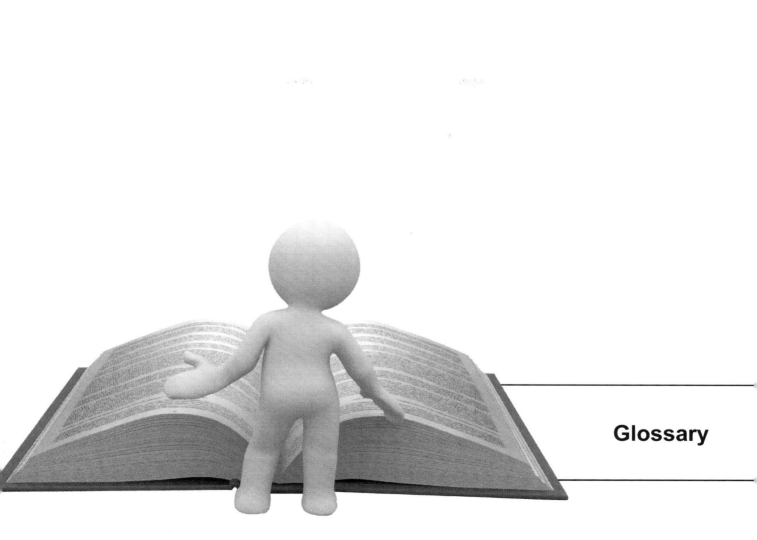

Glossary

Glossary

ADULT LEARNING THEORY
The idea that adults need to recognize the significance and purpose of the material they learn so they can learn it most effectively.

ANDRAGOGY
Theory of adult learning that says that adult learners are self-directed, purpose-oriented, internally motivated, and desire relevancy.

ARCS MODEL OF MOTIVATIONAL DESIGN
Instructional system for designing overall instruction or individual course assignments that emphasizes that students must value the task and believe they can achieve it.

ASSESSMENT TOOLS
Methods instructors use to satisfy instructional objectives (e.g., discussion forums, essays, and exams).

ASYNCHRONOUS
One-way electronic communication (e.g., discussion forums that allow users to post and read messages at any time).

ATTENTION
Aspect of the ARCS Model of Motivational Design that says assignments should capture students' interest, stimulate inquiry, and maintain students' attention.

BLENDED COURSE See *Hybrid course*.

CLOSED-SOURCE LEARNING MANAGEMENT SYSTEM
Proprietary software that you must pay to use and cannot customize without authorization.

CONFIDENCE
Aspect of the ARCS Model of Motivational Design that says assignments should set success expectations, success opportunities, and personal responsibility for students.

CONTENT MANAGEMENT SYSTEM (CMS)
Web-based system that instructors can use to create, store, and deliver content but does not contain features related to instruction, assessment, or grades; used primarily for hybrid or face-to-face courses.

COPYRIGHT
Legal protection for original creators.

COPYRIGHT COMPLIANCE
An institution's efforts to obey copyright laws; institutions may have a copyright compliance officer, a copyright policy, or both.

COPYRIGHT HOLDER
One who has certain exclusive privileges to reproduce, distribute, perform, and display his or her creations.

COPYRIGHT POLICY
General statement of compliance with copyright law that recognizes that the law places several limitations on the copyright holder's rights and how these rights and limitations pertain to distance learning issues.

COURSE DESCRIPTION
Element of a syllabus that contains a summary statement or paragraph about the nature of the course and that matches the course description in the institution's catalog.

COURSE MAPPING
Using the syllabus as a blueprint for developing course topics, resources, content, and activities.

COURSE METHODOLOGY
Element of a syllabus that refers to how the course approaches student learning and lists the various learning methods, including readings, case studies, tests, quizzes, and discussions.

COURSE OBJECTIVES
Elements of a syllabus that detail the specific, measurable, clear, and related goals of the course as they pertain to student performance; also referred to as course outcomes.

COURSE PACKS
Books or articles that publishers allow schools to copy and distribute in educational contexts for a fee and for a limited amount of time (e.g., one semester).

COURSE POLICIES
Element of a syllabus that addresses attendance, make-up examinations, academic dishonesty, accommodations for students who have disabilities, and withdrawal from course enrollment.

COURSE RESOURCES
Supplemental materials designed for use as reference points that affect course-wide materials; examples include discussion rubrics and project templates.

COURSE ROAD MAP
A table that identifies each lesson and states each lesson's objectives and activities that an instructor must develop for the course.

COURSE SHELL
The layout of a course on a learning management system in which instructors can divide courses according to weeks, modules, topics, or content area.

CREATIVE COMMONS
Organization that offers several license types to copyright holders that allow for free distribution of content bearing that license type.

DIRECT INSTRUCTION
Teaching method in which the instructor delivers information and outlines directions for attaining certain competencies; most commonly used instructional strategy.

DUNN AND DUNN LEARNING STYLE MODEL
Model that suggests that five key dimensions (i.e., environmental, emotional, sociological, physiological, and psychological) differentiate learning styles.

EXCLUSIVE AGREEMENT
Agreement in which only one person has the right to use a copyrighted work.

EXPERIENTIAL INSTRUCTION
Teaching method that focuses on the process of learning rather than the result of learning; characterized by an inductive, activity-oriented, learner-centered learning environment.

FAIR USE DOCTRINE
Law that permits limited use of copyrighted works for education, criticism, commentary, news reporting, scholarship, and research without requiring the permission of or payment to the copyright owner.

FLEXIBLE ASSIGNMENTS
Assignments that instructors can reuse for a number of years and across different platforms without needing to perform significant revision.

GRADE COMPUTATION
Element of a syllabus that shows how different assessments are weighted for students' overall grade.

GRADING CRITERIA
Element of a syllabus that gives students clear guidelines for how to complete the coursework.

HYBRID COURSE
Course that blends online and face-to-face delivery, has a substantial proportion of the content delivered online, typically uses online discussions, and has a reduced number of face-to-face meetings.

HYPERTEXT MARKUP LANGUAGE (HTML)
Code that structures tags to lay out information as Web pages.

INDEPENDENT STUDY
Self-study or study within small groups.

INDIRECT INSTRUCTION
Teaching method that focuses on student involvement and problem solving and for which the instructor has more of a facilitator role.

INFORMATION PROCESSING-BASED LEARNING STYLE
Learning theory that evaluates students' cognitive approaches to comprehending and incorporating information and differentiates the way students may sense, perceive, solve problems, organize, and remember information.

INSTITUTIONAL OBLIGATIONS
TEACH Act requirements that institutions be responsible for copyright compliance by imposing their own restrictions on access, developing new policies, and disseminating copyright information.

INSTRUCTIONAL DESIGNER
The member of an online course team who manages course production and suggests options regarding course materials that instructors may not have considered while writing the course.

INSTRUCTIONAL PROCESS
The method used to deliver instruction.

INSTRUCTIONAL OBJECTIVE
Measurable student objective; what an instructor considers satisfactory student performance.

INSTRUCTIONAL VALUE
The measure of how important different pieces of content are to students in grasping course objectives or subobjectives.

INSTRUCTOR INFORMATION
Element of a syllabus that includes the instructor's name, email address, phone number, and office hours.

INTELLECTUAL PROPERTY
Ideas or concepts transformed into a fixed, tangible form.

INTERACTIVE INSTRUCTION
Environment of discussion and sharing between the instructor and students as well as among individual students.

INTERNAL MOTIVATORS
Factors such as self-esteem, social status, and self-satisfaction that motivate adult learners to learn.

JSTOR
Popular online resource for locating scholarly articles that most university and college libraries are licensed to use.

KOLB EXPERIENTIAL LEARNING THEORY
Experiential learning style model whereby learning is a continuous process that involves (in sequential order) concrete experience, reflective observation, abstract conceptualization, and active experimentation.

LEARNING CONTENT MANAGEMENT SYSTEM (LCMS)
Web-based system that stores learning objects that instructors can arrange and use for multiple courses without re-creating each learning object.

LEARNING MANAGEMENT SYSTEM (LMS)
Web-based system that enables instructors to create, deliver, and facilitate online courses without the help of any other software or database.

LEARNING OBJECTS
Content that comprises a course, including assignments and assessments in a variety of visual and audio formats.

LEARNING RESOURCES
Instructional materials designed to confer knowledge and that are typically used in an online course as an equivalent replacement for face-to-face lectures.

LEARNING STYLE
One's preferred method of gathering, organizing, and thinking about information; one's approach to the processing of information.

MINIMUM TECHNOLOGY KNOWLEDGE
Computer skills that students must have to take a course.

MODULAR ASSIGNMENTS
Assignments that allow instructors to update, edit, change, or delete assignments without affecting other course materials and that do not reference materials in a manner that suggests their placement or order in a course.

MODULAR CONTENT
Collection of learning resource. developed as a single learning object.

MODULAR COURSE DESIGN
An online course built using a collection of learning objects.

MULTIDIMENSIONAL/INSTRUCTIONAL-BASED LEARNING STYLE
Learning theory that evaluates the type of learning environment students want.

NONEXCLUSIVE AGREEMENT
Agreement in which more than one person has the right to use a copyrighted work.

ONLINE COURSE
Course in which most or all of the content is delivered online and typically has no face-to-face meetings.

ONLINE COURSE ASSIGNMENTS
Assignments that are specific, flexible, and modular so they work well in an online course.

OPEN CONTENT
Content that is free for public distribution without exclusive rights and exists as a community resource for the masses to use, reuse, and improve.

OPEN-SOURCE LEARNING MANAGEMENT SYSTEM
Web-based system that you can run free of charge and modify to create a more customized platform for delivering instruction.

OVERPERSONALIZATION
Making a course too specific to a certain instructor, term, or institution so that others cannot easily reuse the course.

PEDAGOGY
The art and science of helping children learn.

PERSONALITY-BASED LEARNING STYLE
Learning theory that analyzes the impact of students' personalities on their approach to incorporating information.

PUBLIC DOMAIN
Pertains to works that have either an expired copyright or no copyright restrictions; also called copyleft.

PURPOSE-ORIENTED
The idea that adult learners have either professional or personal goals when they enroll in a particular program or course.

RELEVANCE
Aspect of the ARCS Model of Motivational Design that says assignments should relate to students' goals, match their interests, and tie to their experiences.

RELEVANCY
The idea that adult learners need to know why they are learning something and how it might add value to their lives.

REVISED BLOOM'S TAXONOMY
A hierarchical classification of verbs designed to assist in the development of cognitive-based instruction.

SATISFACTION
Aspect of the ARCS Model of Motivational Design that says assignments should facilitate intrinsic satisfaction, rewarding outcomes, and fair treatment.

SCAFFOLDING
A process that provides students with a structure for learning that reinforces their existing knowledge and helps them explore new information through self-motivation.

SCHOLARLY PUBLISHING STANDARDS
Stipulations that require published scholarly works to communicate clearly and to be unbiased and formatted properly.

SELF-DIRECTED
The idea that the online learning environment is learner-centered as opposed to teacher-directed.

SPECIFIC ASSIGNMENTS
Assignments that require little to no additional direction from instructors.

SUBJECT MATTER EXPERT (SME)
Someone who is an expert in a particular field.

SUBOBJECTIVES
Course objectives broken down into smaller objectives that determine what each lesson should teach and assess.

SYLLABUS
Podium from which the instructor communicates his or her policies and those of the institution along with due dates and any other course requirements.

SYNCHRONOUS
Sessions in which instructors and students engage at the same time, as with face-to-face or chat room sessions.

TEACHING METHODS
Methods instructors use to advance instructional processes (e.g., readings and video materials).

TECHNOLOGIST
The member of an online course team who builds a course on the online platform and who may also create different media pieces for the course.

TECHNOLOGY, EDUCATION, AND COPYRIGHT HARMONIZATION (TEACH) ACT
A law that increased the number and types of copyrighted works an instructor can use without obtaining permission, paying licensing fees, or relying on items in the public domain.

TRANSFORMATIVE USE
Use that involves a changed or modified form of the original copyrighted work.

U.S. COPYRIGHT OFFICE
Federal agency that contains public records of copyright expirations and renewals.

ULRICH'S PERIODICALS DIRECTORY
Comprehensive and widely used database of scholarly journals and periodicals.

UPLOAD
Feature of a learning management system that allows students to electronically deliver work to their instructors.

VARK MODEL
Sensory learning style model that focuses on visual, aural, reading and writing, and kinesthetic learning methods.

VIRTUAL CLASSROOM
Software, such as Adobe Connect, that provides real-time voice or streaming video and allows instructors to deliver live lectures as they would in a traditional classroom.

VIRTUAL LEARNING ENVIRONMENT (VLE)
Another term for learning management system; term used primarily in the United Kingdom and other European countries.

WEB-FACILITATED COURSE
Course that uses Web-based technology to facilitate what is essentially a face-to-face course; may use a course management system or Web pages to post the syllabus and assignments.

WYSIWYG EDITOR
Feature of a learning management system that allows instructors to create content pages directly in the learning management system instead of uploading external text documents.

38410606R10083

Made in the USA
Lexington, KY
07 January 2015